Road Signs
for the Journey

Road Signs
for the Journey

A Profile of Mennonite Church USA

Conrad L. Kanagy

Herald Press
Scottdale, Pennsylvania
Waterloo, Ontario

Library of Congress Cataloging-in-Publication Data
Kanagy, Conrad L.
  Road signs for the journey : a profile of Mennonite Church /
Conrad L. Kanagy.
      p. cm.
  Includes bibliographical references.
  ISBN 978-0-8361-9375-6 (pbk. : alk. paper)
  1. Mennonite Church USA. I. Title.
  BX8121.3.K36 2007
  289.7'73—dc22
                                    2007008965

ROAD SIGNS FOR THE JOURNEY
Copyright © 2007 by Herald Press, Scottdale, Pa. 15683
  Published simultaneously in Canada by Herald Press,
  Waterloo, Ont. N2L 6H7. All rights reserved
Library of Congress Catalog Card Number: 2007008965
International Standard Book Number: 978-0-8361-9375-6
Printed in the United States of America
Book design by Sandra Johnson
Graphics by Joseph Hollinger
Cover by Ingrid Hess

12 11 10 09 08   10 9 8 7 6 5 4 3

To order or request information please call 1-800-245-7894
or visit www.heraldpress.com.

To my maternal grandparents,
Erie "Pap" and Verna Renno,
whose lives and ministry always reflected Jesus.

Contents

Foreword by John D. Roth 9
Preface 11

1. Road Signs and Guideposts 19
2. God's People Then 33
3. God's People Now 45
4. The Call 67
5. God's Words—Then and Now 89
6. Homeland Security 111
7. 587 BC—The Fall 135
8. Exiled in Babylon 157
9. Journeying Toward God's Reign 175

Notes 195
Bibliography 201
The Author 205

Foreword

Religious sociologists in the United States disagree about many things. But on one point they are in almost complete accord: traditional forms of denominational loyalty are undergoing a profound transformation. With the notable exception of some Baptist and Pentecostal groups, virtually all of the mainstream Protestant churches are in decline—struggling to cope with aging memberships, shrinking budgets, blurred theological identity, and waning allegiance to church traditions. To be sure, most Americans continue to define themselves as "religious" or "spiritual," but they are less and less inclined to frame their religious identity within denominational categories or to remain loyal to a single denomination throughout their entire lives.

Mennonites, of course, have long taken a certain pride in being "a people apart." Traditionally, practices like nonresistance, church discipline, mutual aid, and simplicity have kept them slightly out-of-step with the dominant forms of public Christianity. But as Conrad Kanagy makes abundantly clear in the troubling book you are about to read, this self-image may no longer square with reality. On the basis of Kanagy's recent survey data, the Mennonite Church USA is now facing virtually all of the same challenges amply documented among the larger Protestant denominations.

Like a surgeon wielding a scalpel, Kanagy lays bare a host of painful facts about the current state of Mennonite affairs. With the exception of a growing number of "racial/ethnic" congregations, the average age of Mennonite Church USA members is rising, while overall membership is declining. Compared with the results of a similar survey in 1989, Mennonites today are less able to articulate theological distinctives, they are less inclined to support conference and denominational leadership, and they are more likely to regard Mennonite beliefs as an impediment to the message of the gospel. Despite a strong affirmation for the principle of the missional church, there is little evidence that Mennonites today are all that eager to actually share the gospel with their non-Christian neighbors.

Although the evidence it presents is sometimes painful, *Road Signs for the Journey* is a book that everyone who cares about the future of the church will want to read carefully and ponder well. Like a good physician, Kanagy knows that the path to health and wholeness must begin with a clear appraisal of the symptoms. By framing his analysis within the rich theological language of the prophet Jeremiah, Kanagy consistently moves from the painful truth of our current situation to a reminder that new life can indeed spring from unexpected sources—woven into his sociological analysis are some surprising seeds of hope. Ultimately, God desires that we respond in faithfulness to his call. But since that response always finds expression in particular forms—the cultural matrix of specific beliefs and concrete practices—Christians will inevitably find themselves aligning with denominations of one sort or another. The challenge ahead for the Mennonite Church USA is to align ourselves with God's unsettling and surprising movement in the world while also being faithful stewards of a "goodly heritage" (Psalm 16:6 NRSV).

Framing the challenge in this way does not diminish the need for Mennonite leaders to respond urgently and creatively to the difficult facts Kanagy presents in *Road Signs for the Journey*. But it does mean that the outcome of that response—the future of the Mennonite Church USA—rests finally in God's hands rather than our own.

It is my prayer that a generation from now, a revived and stronger Mennonite church will look back on this book not only as a wake-up call but also as a road map that pointed the way to a more faithful identity.

John D. Roth
Goshen College
April 2007

Preface

I first learned about the Church Member Profile projects while an undergraduate sociology major at Wheaton College in the mid-1980s. At that point, J. Howard Kauffman, Leland Harder, and Leo Driedger were making plans for a profile they would conduct in 1989. It would follow up an earlier one released in 1972. I recall imagining what fun it would be to participate in such a project some day.

Later in the 1990s, while teaching at Elizabethtown College, I authored several publications (including one with Leo Driedger) using data from these earlier profiles. At that time, my research in the sociology of religion was largely geared toward the academy and scholarly journals.

All of that changed, however, when our congregation—Elizabethtown Mennonite—called me to serve as lead pastor in the year 2000. While I continued to teach at the college, I discontinued my academic writing and research. A few months after being ordained, I was diagnosed with papillary thyroid cancer. While usually quite treatable, mine was more resistant than most. After three years it remained, despite multiple surgeries and treatments. But tests prior to another scheduled treatment in late 2003 revealed that all evidence of the disease was gone, a result for which we give God the glory!

Almost immediately I felt a desire to return to writing. In early 2004, Donald B. Kraybill and I began conversations about the possibility of a third member profile that would build on the earlier work of Kauffman, Harder, and Driedger. Because those profiles had been sponsored in part by Mennonite Mutual Aid, we began with an initial inquiry to Howard Brenneman (then president of MMA). Howard's enthusiastic response and vision for the project led to the development of a formal proposal to Mennonite Church USA. The proposal was graciously received and supported by Mennonite Church USA Executive Board and its churchwide agencies (including a major grant from MMA). Others who provided financial support included Mennonite Central Committee, Mennonite Disaster Service, Goodville Mutual and Casualty Company, the Schowalter Foundation, Mennonite Financial Services, Eastern Mennonite Missions, and several private contributors.

Church Member Profile 2006 was composed of three denominations—Mennonite Church USA, the Church of the Brethren, and the Brethren in Christ. Donald B. Kraybill was the overall project director, while each denomination had a separate director—Carl D. Bowman of Bridgewater College for the Church of the Brethren, Ronald Burwell of Messiah College for the Brethren in Christ, and myself for Mennonite Church USA. This book reports only findings from members of Mennonite Church USA.

There are many persons to thank for their support and participation in this project. While I cannot name everyone, they include:

- Nearly one hundred churchwide agency leaders, area conference leaders, pastors, and scholars who met in consultations to brainstorm about the project and possible topics that should be included in the questionnaire.
- Many volunteers (most from the Elizabethtown Church of the Brethren) who stamped and stuffed thousands of envelopes and carried out other important tasks.
- An incredibly competent support staff at the Young Center led by Dawn Houff and Erin Lichti. Their day-to-day management of the project was flawless.
- Tara Fagan who was responsible for cleaning the data, preparing it for analysis, and conducting some of the preliminary analyses.
- Don Kraybill, friend, colleague, and mentor for fourteen years, who gave direction and oversight to this project with an expertise and eye for detail like few others. While all four directors contributed to the writing of the questionnaire, Don in particular poured himself into the details of its development.

- Carl Bowman, whose sociological expertise and collegial participation strengthened the overall design of the project for all three denominations.
- Nearly three thousand members of Mennonite congregations—including a special sample of Racial/Ethnic members and a special sample of pastors—who completed a questionnaire.
- Project partners Yvonne Platts, Freeman Miller, Rodolfo Jimenez, and Valentina Satvedi who facilitated the involvement of twenty-one Racial/Ethnic congregations in Philadelphia, Chicago, and Los Angeles.
- Laura Livengood, whose administrative assistance was helpful in the development of the book and congregational resources.
- A team of six members of Elizabethtown Mennonite Church who patiently read and insightfully responded to early drafts of this book: Roy Wert, Susan Hochstedler, James Lutz, Ron Kratz, Iris Martin, and Josh Gish.
- Three pastors who served as consultants to the development of a set of congregational resources related to the book and who continually encouraged me in the work: Leonard Dow (Oxford Circle Mennonite Church), Judy Zook (New Holland Mennonite Church), and Stan Shantz (James Street Mennonite Church).
- Levi Miller and Michael Degan of Herald Press. Their editorial direction and support was deeply appreciated and kept the book on a timely track.
- Joseph Hollinger of OpenRoutes Media who created hundreds of slides for presentations to Mennonite Church USA leaders as well as graphics for the book.
- Mennonite Church USA Executive Board members, Constituency Leaders Council members, and churchwide agency leaders who listened to presentations of the data, asked important questions, and offered helpful perspectives from their own positions and experiences in the church.
- J. Ron Byler, associate director of Mennonite Church USA, with whom I worked on a regular basis throughout the project. Ron's engagement and interest in the project opened numerous doors for dissemination of the data. I came to greatly appreciate and value his affirmation and encouragement throughout our collaboration.

- Jim Schrag, executive director of Mennonite Church USA, who was always supportive of the project and keenly interested in both the numbers and their meaning. Both Jim and Ron approached the data with an attitude of listening, reflecting, and asking insightful questions. Their commitment to the project and the seriousness with which they approached the data contradict the comment I once heard from a nationally known research director that denominational leaders never pay attention to social science data.

In January 2005 I took a personal retreat to pray about this project. During that day, I sensed a nudge to turn to Jeremiah 31, and in doing so discovered verse 21, where God commands the people of Israel to set up "road signs; put up guideposts" to direct them on their journey back from exile. From that day on, I began to think of Mennonite Member Profile 2006 as a set of road signs and guideposts by which God could reveal where members of Mennonite Church USA are on our journey and where God might be pointing us. This notion of road signs and guideposts has shaped my thinking about the significance of the project and influenced the writing of this book in particular.

There are many ways that one can view the church today. My own perspective is that of a sociologist and pastor. My goal in this book is to communicate with persons in the pew more so than with scholars and academics. This book is not an analysis primarily of Mennonite Church USA as a denominational organization or of its congregations. Rather, it is a study of members of the denomination and their social and spiritual location at the beginning of the twenty-first century.

In the book I rely on the biblical narrative of Jeremiah as a frame around which to raise questions about God's people today and against which to discuss the findings of Mennonite Member Profile 2006. Doing so has likely contributed to a kind of "edginess" to the book—one should probably expect such when hanging out with Old Testament prophets too long! But I fully recognize that the challenges in this book are as much for me as for anyone who reads it, and I trust that I have been shaped by its message in ways that I pray it will also shape the perspectives of others. Throughout the book I highlight the importance of the growing number of Racial/Ethnic members and congregations who are part of Mennonite Church USA. The past three years of working on this project have provided me with opportunities to visit many of these congregations and to meet with their pastors. I have become painfully aware of how little I knew about these brothers and sisters and of their reality prior to this project. Despite being an ordained minister in the denomination with them and despite being a trained sociologist who has taught about race and ethnic relations, I had almost no awareness of Racial/Ethnic members in my own church. I had no relationships with them as brothers and sisters in Christ, no understanding of their feelings of marginalization within the church, and no sense of the realities within which they live. In my many conversations with white members over the past three years, it is clear that my own lack of awareness and understanding is widespread in the broader church.

My hope and prayer is that this book will help to foster a conversation across racial and ethnic lines that will be honest and constructive. Many African-American, Asian, and Hispanic/Latino Mennonites have shared their lives with me over the past three years and have been transparent in expressing both the pain and joy they experience in being Mennonite Christians. As you will hear me say throughout this book, I believe that the renewal of the church and the coming of God's kingdom depends on overcoming the sins of racism that remain in the church and in creating communities that understand and practice reconciliation grounded in the life and death of Jesus Christ.

While the tone of my writing portrays despair at times, I trust that it does not betray two fundamental beliefs that I hold—one theological and one sociological. First, as a sociologist I teach my students that human beings are *and* are not victims of the social and cultural worlds we live in. While these worlds are given to us at birth, and while they have tremendous power to shape us, they were created by other human beings before us. As a result, we too have power to shape our own worlds and the worlds of those who will come after us. In other words, we can change and we can influence change in others. But too often we deny the reality of our worlds, because doing so is too painful or anxiety-producing. Such denial, however, usually means that we will never attempt the constructive changes needed in our personal lives, families, churches, and communities. I trust this book, though challenging at times, will reveal some of what needs changed in our worlds if we are going to be faithful followers of Jesus Christ.

Second, I believe that God is moving and that God's reign is on the way. This movement depends on us even while at the same time not depending on us at all. Such a paradox parallels the mystery of God's kingdom, which is "here" but "not yet." The reign of God, ushered in by the life, death, and resurrection of Jesus Christ, is approaching, and it will overcome history regardless of whether we or history are ready for it.

At the same time, I do believe that we have a critical role to play if that kingdom is to be received in our families, churches, and neighborhoods. Just like those to whom Jesus sent the seventy-two in Luke 10, we can receive the shalom of the kingdom, or we can resist it. If we resist, we will have missed our chance to greet the kingdom. Nevertheless, it has "come near." While I argue that the circumstances of our lives (idolatry, apathy, affluence) in many ways reflect the reality of God's people in the sixth century BC, God's plan even then was shalom and the kingdom. The coming of Jesus Christ between then and now only means that we are that much closer to the reality of that grand day!

Of all those persons who have supported this project, I am most grateful to my wife, Heidi, and our son, Jacob, for their love, care, and patience throughout the past three years. Little did they or I know the amount of work that was in store when I resigned as pastor to take on this project. Traveling too much and writing for too many hours often meant that my year off from teaching felt less like a "sabbatical" than we had imagined. But in the middle of the day, Heidi and I often took a much needed walk followed by a cup of coffee together. Heidi's continual intercession and her commitment to being a spiritual center in our home has gotten both Jacob and I through more tight squeezes than we will ever know. And whether it was going out for breakfast, playing tennis, ping pong, or skiing, the moments I spent with Jacob, who is now a senior in high school, were always treasured moments. His humor, shared in stories about work and school, kept me in stitches and prevented me from taking myself too seriously. These moments with Heidi and Jacob refreshed my heart and mind and kept me grounded in God's reality. I am so grateful for their love and companionship, which are wrapped into these pages as much as is my own life.

Finally, I thank God for the leading and direction of the Holy Spirit throughout this project, and the many ways in which the Spirit's presence was shown over these past three years of work.

Conrad L. Kanagy
Elizabethtown, Pennsylvania
April 2007

1

Road Signs and Guideposts

This is what the LORD says: "Stand at the crossroads and look; ask for the ancient paths, ask where the good way is, and walk in it, and you will find rest for your souls. But you said, 'We will not walk in it.'" —Jeremiah 6:16

Yet my people have forgotten me; they burn incense to worthless idols, which made them stumble in their ways and in the ancient paths. They made them walk in bypaths and on roads not built up. —Jeremiah 18:15

"Set up road signs; put up guideposts. Take note of the highway, the road that you take. Return, O Virgin Israel, return to your towns." —Jeremiah 31:21

Ancient paths of safety and security, good ways of life and rest— these were God's promises from the time of Abraham and Sarah to the days of Jeremiah. But through the centuries, the people of God consistently followed their own paths, choosing shortcuts that led nowhere and building highways that brought terror and destruction. This tug of war between God and God's people reached a climax in the sixth century BC when the forces of Babylon destroyed Jerusalem, ransacked the temple, and took thousands of Judah's citizens to Babylon. Exile was the detour for an unwillingness to choose God's ways.

But consistent with God's character, Yahweh remained in compassionate and desperate pursuit, beckoning the children of Israel back to the ancient paths. Anticipating their return from exile, God instructed the people to erect "road signs" and "guideposts" to keep them from getting off track again and to ensure that their feet would remain steadfastly on the ancient paths and good ways.

Early in 2006, more than three thousand members of Mennonite congregations across the United States received a seventeen-page questionnaire by mail asking about their religious beliefs and practices, values, lifestyle choices, church participation, evangelism efforts, and much more.[1] Additional questionnaires were distributed to a special sample of Racial/Ethnic members in three urban areas and to five hundred ordained Mennonite ministers.

Called Mennonite Member Profile 2006, the study's broad sampling of congregations and individuals, Racial/Ethnic groups, and church leaders makes it the most comprehensive survey ever of "mainstream" Mennonites in the United States. Magnifying its importance are two earlier surveys, conducted in 1972 and 1989 that permit a thirty-five-year window from which to view changes among Mennonites in the United States.[2]

The responses of members in Mennonite Member Profile 2006 represent, in part, road signs and guideposts for God's people today—markers that reveal whether we are on the ancient paths and good ways or taking shortcuts and detours of our own making.

Research Approach

In the summer of 2005, 124 Mennonite congregations were selected from the Mennonite Church USA database of 965 congregations.[3] A scientific selection process ensured that members chosen from these congregations would be representative of all members in the denomination.[4]

Using membership directories from participating congregations, members eighteen years of age and older were randomly selected to receive a survey. This process yielded a database of 3,080 members.[5] Mennonite Member Profile 2006 was mailed on February 14, 2006. By early summer of the same year, 76% of respondents had returned useable questionnaires for a total number of 2,216 responses.[6]

Racial/Ethnic sample. In comparison to other U.S. denominations, Mennonite Church USA has a large number of Racial/Ethnic congregations and members. The term "Racial/Ethnic" is a self-designation by groups with members who are African-American, Latino/Hispanic, Asian, Native American, and of other "other than Anglo" origin. At least 18% (169 congregations) of Mennonite Church USA congregations are Racial/Ethnic and their members account for nearly 11% of the denomination's membership.[7]

Racial/Ethnic persons are typically underrepresented in social science research, and particularly in survey research. This was true in the member profiles in 1972 and 1989, both of which included too few Racial/Ethnic members to conduct any meaningful analysis. Because of this historic under representation, Mennonite Member Profile 2006 included a special sample of Racial/Ethnic members in three urban areas: Philadelphia, Chicago, and Los Angeles.[8]

Pastor sample. Five hundred active and active without charge Mennonite ministers also received a full-length member questionnaire. Three hundred and nineteen ministers returned a completed profile for a response rate of 65%. Responses from pastors will be included in some of the analyses in this book.[9]

Member Responses

Members reacted in different ways to the invitation to complete a questionnaire. Some expressed gratitude for the opportunity to reflect on their lives and their church, such as this comment from a fifty-something construction engineer in the Midwest:

> I sincerely appreciate the opportunity to ask the hard questions of myself, my faith community and church, to reflect and discuss, without being summarily dismissed or condemned.

A few resented what they perceived to be the motivation for the questionnaire, such as this thirty-something father of four from the southeastern United States:

> Surveys to determine "where people are" reflect the moral incompetence of the Mennonite Church. Leadership directed

by God's word *should* move people to where God intends them to be. If you don't know where God intends us to be, you are not a leader but a follower.

Some expressed strong feelings of affection for their church, such as this elderly woman who had been a member of a Mennonite congregation for just two years:

> They are the most caring group of people I've ever encountered, always there for you when a need arises.

Others despaired about their experience of the church, such as this urban artist, no longer active in a Mennonite congregation:

> Mennonites are too insular. They largely ignore some of the greatest achievements of humankind, both in the artistic and in the intellectual world. Or maybe they are scared because it might challenge their beliefs. They don't understand that it is OK—or even good—to question one's fundamental assumptions at any time.

Still others revealed anxieties about the future of the church:

> Mennonites are good, sound, caring people and I think in general we are too satisfied with the status quo and keep to ourselves too much. We need to be able to reach out to the unchurched, even if it means starting a "soup kitchen" for example. There is an awful lot of need out there! We are too happy to just be the same from year to year. If we don't find a way to grow we will surely die out.

Regardless of their feelings about the project or about the church, a response rate of 76% is highly unusual for mail surveys, including denominational surveys, which typically yield no more than a twenty- to thirty-percent response. While data from Mennonite Member Profile 2006 reveal evidence of crisis and disruption within the church and among its members, the response rate suggests that members want to actively engage the church in conversation about their views and perspectives.

So What?

Those who are not professional social scientists—which I am keenly aware is just about everybody—may well wonder why such an effort was made to collect this information and what will become of it anyway. Are such surveys a sign of moral incompetence by church leaders, as the member above suggested?

The question "So what?" was also raised by an African-American pastor when I asked him how the results of Mennonite Member Profile 2006 might be helpful in his urban church. He responded immediately and with passion: "We don't need any more information that doesn't lead to transformation!" His response was consistent with a theme articulated by other urban pastors when I talked with them about the study: "If it's not kingdom work, we're not interested."

More recently I heard the director of a religious research institute, who has worked for decades with national denominations, candidly remark: "As much as I value data and social science methods, I've never yet met a church leader who made a decision based on empirical research. The religious world operates theologically."

All of these persons are raising important questions: (1) Does research represent the moral incompetence of leaders to guide the church? (2) Is social science information able to contribute to spiritual transformation? (3) Can surveys about the church be "kingdom" work or just more distraction from such work? (4) Will pastors and congregation members be able to use the information gathered in Mennonite Member Profile 2006 in any meaningful way?

Throughout the course of this project, these "So what?" questions have haunted as well as motivated both my work and my prayer. In January 2005, as plans for Mennonite Member Profile 2006 were developing, I took a personal retreat to the mountains of my childhood home in Belleville, Pennsylvania. At some point during that day, while praying and journaling, I sensed an impulse to turn to Jeremiah 31. In doing so, I discovered God's instructions to the people of Judah to erect road signs and guideposts for their journey back to Jerusalem from exile in Babylon (see Jeremiah 31:21). These road signs and guideposts were to ensure that God's people not get off track on their way home, as they so often had done throughout their history.

With this verse as a starting point, I began to imagine that

Mennonite Member Profile 2006 might function as do all road signs and guideposts—to show the traveler where he or she is on the journey and to point out new directions that may be warranted. In this way, the purpose of this book is twofold:

- To show the location—spiritual, political, theological, social, and more—of Mennonites in the United States at the beginning of the twenty-first century, making comparisons with earlier Mennonites, with other U.S. Christians, and with God's expectations for his people as reflected in the book of Jeremiah.
- To suggest new directions that Mennonites may want to consider on their journey toward the reign of God.

Made Relevant by God's Word

Understanding these purposes, I continued to wrestle with the question of how to speak the sociological truth about where we are as Mennonites today within a framework that reflects God's eternal reality. In this struggle I found myself drawn again to the book of Jeremiah, not simply for the metaphor of road signs and guideposts, but as a biblical narrative out of which to discuss the findings of Mennonite Member Profile 2006.

In doing so, I hope to address the concerns of the urban pastor who had no interest in information without transformation, and of the respondent who believes that social science surveys are a sign of morally incompetent leadership, and of the religious research director who bemoaned the irrelevance of social science data to church leaders whose frameworks are largely theological. Placing this project within the biblical story of Jeremiah moves Mennonite Member Profile 2006 from an academic exercise of curiosity to a spiritual inquiry of looking for God's presence and direction among God's people today.

Jeremiah

If we remember him at all, most of us know Jeremiah as a prophet or preacher. Few of us think of him as the keen social observer and analyst that he was. Jeremiah, like all true prophets, accurately identified the social, political, economic, and spiritual realities of God's people. And more than anyone else in his day, Jeremiah was willing to speak the truth about those realities—that God's people were an idolatrous and disobedient people whom God was about to judge.[10] Though unpopular on all accounts with just about everybody, Jeremiah courageously pointed out the sin of God's people, predicted the destruction of Jerusalem and the temple, and prophesied a new day of shalom. In other words, his words served as road signs and guideposts.

The reader should be aware of several perspectives that I bring to this book, nurtured in my research as a sociologist of religion, my experience as a pastor, and as a consultant to congregations across several denominations.

A Church in Crisis

I believe that the church in North America is in crisis, or at least in the midst of significant disruption, and that without spiritual renewal and transformation it will become increasingly irrelevant. Of the seven churches in the book of Revelation that Christ addresses a century after his death and resurrection, I believe that the North American church is most like Laodicea—wealthy, healthy, and well dressed, but in Jesus' own words "wretched, pitiful, poor, blind and naked" (Revelation 3:17). The North American church is poised between the declining church of postmodern Europe and the rapid growth of the church in the global south (Asia, Latin America, and Africa).

I am by no means the first or only person saying this. In fact, there has been a growing crescendo of voices over the past several decades making this kind of claim—from the religious left and the right, among Protestant mainliners and evangelicals, by theologians, historians, pastors, and social scientists. All are saying a similar thing—that the church in North America is in decline, a decline that can be measured by numbers of members as well as by other qualitative indicators of spiritual vitality. Walter Brueggemann, a leading Old Testament theologian, puts it this way:

> My sense is that the ministry of the American church is in many ways fatigued and close to despair. That is so because we are double-minded. On the one hand, we have some glimpses of the truth of God's gospel. . . . On the other hand, the church is so fully enmeshed in the dominant values of our culture that freedom for action is difficult. In any case, it is evident that ministry will be freed of fatigue, despair, and cynicism only as we are able to see clearly what we are up to, and then perhaps able to act intentionally.[11]

Darrell Guder, missional theologian and teacher sounds a similar theme:

> The crises are certainly many and complex: diminishing numbers, clergy burnout, the loss of youth, the end of denominational loyalty, biblical illiteracy, divisions in the ranks . . . the irrelevance of traditional forms of worship, the loss of genuine spirituality, and widespread confusion about both the purpose and the message of the church of Jesus Christ.[12]

The crisis in the church has led to increased conflicts between Christians on the right and the left, and between mainline Protestants and evangelicals. In this conflict, Protestant evangelicals too often embrace a "God and country" civil religion that diminishes the transformative power of the gospel, while Protestant mainliners emphasize the need for social justice without addressing personal salvation and individual transformation through Jesus Christ.[13]

In turning to politics as the primary vehicle for social change, evangelicals have abandoned the costly requirements of the cross, compromised the truth of the gospel, and created questionable alliances with political leaders and movements. Even while preaching against particular sins such as homosexuality and abortion, evangelicals have become ever more like those they most oppose in other lifestyle choices, all the while abandoning the poor and needy on the margins of society.

Mainline Protestants, on the other hand, have often placed their emphasis on a social gospel that cares for the poor and protests social injustice but ignores the power of Jesus Christ to overcome sin in both social structures and individual lives. The mainline equation, like the evangelical one, too often depends on political solutions while omitting the whole truth that Jesus Christ came to transform all of creation—nature, society, and individuals—by his life, death, and resurrection.

As Mennonites who sometimes profess a "third way," we face the tension of being pulled to one side or other of the theological and cultural debate I have just described.[14] Our difficulty in managing the polarities of these culture wars has silenced our unique and historic witness as a people of God who—in word and deed—proclaim the gospel's power to transform both structures and individuals. John Roth, Mennonite historian and advocate for a "sabbatical" from party politics among Mennonites defines this struggle of Mennonites today: "Our increasing readiness to identify ourselves as Republicans and Democrats . . . and our inability to distinguish our political witness from our deeply entrenched red/blue divide is an embarrassment to the church."[15]

In visiting Mennonite congregations in the United State today, one is sometimes hard pressed to know exactly what Mennonites believe and practice. Anabaptists have become, in some ways, collections of persons with no identifiable home, lost without a sense of what distinguishes us from evangelical and mainline, from right and left, and from the broader society. One pastor who I interviewed described his congregation as one made up of separate groups, each drinking from different theological streams who "worship together in the same space but never really talk to one another." In fact, they seem to prefer it that way: "After a congregational meeting in which members were encouraged to discuss a controversial topic, one member stated that he/she liked it better not knowing what others in the congregation believed about issues that might divide them."

The Middle and the Margins

Some may be surprised by my use of the book of Jeremiah as the biblical narrative around which to organize a sociological analysis of Mennonites today. I do so as one who believes that the Old

Testament, seen through the life and teachings of Jesus, offers a prophetic challenge that many of us would prefer to forget. Spending time in Jeremiah has strengthened my conviction about the need and opportunity for Mennonites to give a prophetic witness today—to boldly proclaim God's plans and purposes to the world. But like all prophetic voices, this witness comes most effectively from those whose lives contrast with the values and lifestyle of the larger culture and society—who intentionally challenge the dominant cultural narrative. In other words, prophetic voices are most often from the margins of society, from those alienated, disenfranchised, and devalued by those in the middle.

Biblical examples of such prophetic responses from the margins include Jeremiah, John the Baptist, and Jesus himself. Any relevant and effective call to follow Jesus rarely comes from those in the middle of society—those focused on protecting their power, status, control, and affluence. While Mennonites historically shared a place on the margins of the broader culture, it is clear from the data of Mennonite Member Profile 2006 that not many of us—with the exception of Racial/Ethnic members—remain there today. Most Mennonites are more like the broader culture—something our parents and grandparents often referred to as "the world"—than ever before.

Our inability or unwillingness to step away from the comfortable middle where most North American Christians find themselves today is a primary reason that the church (including Mennonites) has lost its prophetic voice. We have stopped speaking the whole truth about Christ to our neighbors, our friends, our communities, the nation, and the world. Too often when we attempt to do so, it is in diluted, popular language that ensures that we and our potential converts won't lose our skin over the deal, that nothing too radical will become of such a decision to follow Jesus.

Brueggemann suggests that those in the middle of society and of the church are "history stoppers" rather than "history makers."[16] History makers, including the prophets, speak on the edges of their culture and society, shouting God's truth to those in the middle—to the "history stoppers" who are too busy preserving their own position and status to bother with God's truth. History stoppers tend to live in denial of God's reality. History makers, by speaking the truth, begin to shape and to put into motion the plans and purposes of God. The radical, off-the-wall words of history makers become the foundation for the new thing that God wants to do. The problem is that most of us in North America have achieved our current status by siding with the history stoppers—preserving our positions and protecting our investments while watering down the truth about our sinful condition and a costly gospel. The church in North America is in desperate need of a few more prophetic history makers and a few less pathetic history stoppers.

As you will hear me repeat frequently throughout this book, I believe that Racial/Ethnic members in Mennonite Church USA hold a key to recovering the prophetic witness of Mennonites today. In terms of power, position, and privilege, African-Americans, Native Americans, Latino/Hispanics, Asians, and other Racial/Ethnic Mennonites remain on the margins both of the denomination and of American society. By living out of a context of marginalization, Racial/Ethnic members have a perspective of the church, of the world, and of God that those in the middle desperately need to hear and to learn from. White, affluent Mennonites in North America are increasingly removed from these margins, having become more assimilated, secure, and comfortable than ever before. According to one leader in Mennonite mission efforts, as Mennonites have moved to the middle, they have more difficulty today than in the past identifying with the life experiences of poverty and injustice of those they are called to serve in cross-cultural contexts.

A Missional Response

A church in crisis needs a theology for that crisis. As the pastor of a Mennonite congregation for several years, I found myself troubled by our inability or unwillingness (including my own) to faithfully share the good news of Jesus Christ in both word and deed in our local communities. It was during my pastoral experience that I came to understand, more than any time before, the crisis in which the North American church finds itself: apathy about its membership decline and eventual disappearance, intoxication with its affluence and idols, chronic conflict over doctrinal and theological issues that repeatedly cause it to divide, and continual meddling with organizational structures and technical solutions that rarely change anything of substance. Out of this recognition of failure I felt myself yearning for a theology that both explained the crisis in the church and offered God's response to it.

I believe that the thirty-year discussion of the missional church is a gift of God's Spirit to a church in crisis and represents a powerful theology to address that crisis. Missional church theology is rooted in the writings and experience of Lesslie Newbigin, a long-time missionary to India who returned home to England in the 1970s to find that the culture and society he knew had become largely pagan. The basic claim of missional thinkers is this: The era of "Christendom" is over in the West, and there is no longer a consistent and viable Christian witness to western culture. That is, Christianity no longer has the kind of influence it once had to shape the broader culture and society. The question that haunted Newbigin and that drives missional conversation today remains: "Can the West [Europe and North America] be converted?"[17]

Besides recognizing the disruption and crisis in the church, missional theologians make several other important assumptions.[18] These assumptions are of particular relevance to local congregations if denominations, area conferences, and church agencies have any hope of ever becoming missional.

- Local congregations have unique callings (or vocations) to the communities and neighborhoods that surround them.
- Local congregations must begin to see themselves as church when sent into the world throughout the week as well as when gathered on Sunday morning.
- God was the first missionary to the world and God remains a missionary still. God's heart is always for the world.
- The crisis in the church cannot be fixed by rational, technological solutions or new programs. It will require serious

and critical reflection on values and beliefs about God and the church, and a willingness to address the deep cultural and spiritual problems at the heart of the crisis.

• God is as much at work in the world as in the church, and God's Spirit continually surprises us with activity in places we thought were dry and barren.

• Spiritual discernment led by the Holy Spirit is required if congregations are going to effectively transform their local communities with the gospel.

• Missional renewal can happen only as Christians discern together around God's Word.

These and other assumptions shape my understanding of missional church, and you will see them reflected throughout this book. For I believe that these "missional" truths are biblical truths, deposited by God in eternity and recovered for us today in order to address the deep crisis in the North American church.

Conclusion

By now it should be clear that this book is not just a scholarly report of what was learned about Mennonites in the United State through Mennonite Member Profile 2006. Rather it's an effort to place the findings of a sociological study within the larger eternal story of God and God's people. I am not interested in retelling the biblical story of Jeremiah as information or of reporting sophisticated statistics for the intellectually curious. Some will complain that the book has too little data from Mennonite Member Profile 2006 and too much theological content. Others will lament that it has too much data and not enough theology.

Such is the challenge I have faced in connecting the biblical story—which is the story of all of us—with the sociological reality of God's people today. In this effort I have sensed the Spirit's affirmation and leading. While I do not put myself in the company of prophets such as Jeremiah, Isaiah, Walter Brueggemann, and others, I do understand my task to reflect theirs—to provide some road signs and guideposts for God's people today that might show us where we are and raise questions about where we should be going.

Outline

This book consists of nine chapters. Chapter two outlines the book of Jeremiah and the activity of God, the prophet, and God's people in the sixth century BC. Chapter three provides a profile of Mennonite Church USA members today and compares them with Mennonites thirty-five years ago. Chapters four through nine each address a particular theme from the book of Jeremiah that I connect with findings from Mennonite Member Profile 2006 and, where possible, to the earlier two member profiles.

This book may also be useful in Sunday school class and small group settings. It can be supplemented with a set of congregational resources on CD and DVD entitled *Resources for the Journey: A Profile of Mennonite Church USA.* The set of congregational resources includes:

- sermon outlines
- worship resources
- small group and Sunday school materials
- video excerpts to promote class discussion
- a leader's guide

My prayer is that something in this book will cause you to see and experience in a new way God's plans and purposes for God's people today, particularly that people who in one way or another are connected to the Anabaptist movement that began nearly five hundred years ago. And that in so doing, you will see yourself somewhere in these pages and be able to reflect on the road signs and guideposts in your own life and journey.

2

God's People Then

During the reign of King Josiah, the LORD said to me, "Have you seen what faithless Israel has done? She has gone up on every high hill and under every spreading tree and has committed adultery there. I thought that after she had done all this she would return to me but she did not, and her unfaithful sister Judah saw it. I gave faithless Israel her certificate of divorce and sent her away because of all her adulteries. Yet I saw that her unfaithful sister Judah had no fear; she also went out and committed adultery. Because Israel's immorality mattered so little to her, she defiled the land and committed adultery with stone and wood. In spite of all this, her unfaithful sister Judah did not return to me with all her heart, but only in pretense," declares the LORD. . . .

"How gladly would I treat you like sons and give you a desirable land, and the most beautiful inheritance of any nation." I thought you would call me "Father" and not turn away from following me. . . . But . . . you have been unfaithful to me . . ." declares the LORD. —Jeremiah 3:6-10, 19-20

In the two kingdoms of Israel and Judah—divided after the reign of King Solomon—Israel was the first to forsake Yahweh for the worship of idols and other gods. But Judah soon followed, and both nations chronically abandoned their relationship with their Maker.

Without much success, Jeremiah tried to mediate the dialogue and relationship between God and God's people, pointing out the grievous sins of the people and their pending judgment, while at the same time revealing the heart of Yahweh that would restore and redeem them if they repented.

"I thought you would call me Father," Yahweh weeps, and we

feel God's passion for a people who continually abandon their Maker. These opening verses in chapter three of Jeremiah also capture the ongoing struggle of God's people today. Disobedience, allegiance to things other than God, and abandonment of those on the margins remain our story. The temptation to commit idolatry with the things of this world—power, security, wealth, status, success, possessions, and relationships—too often overcomes us.

And yet, despite our sins and failures, God pleads for us to return to a relationship with him, to again choose the ancient paths, and to again worship the living One rather than idols of our own making. God's call in the seventh and sixth centuries BC came through the faithful prophet Jeremiah and continues to come to us today. But the response of God's people then to Jeremiah's message is more often than not the response of God's people today.

Reading to Listen

In this chapter we will look more closely at the situation of God's people in the sixth century BC, just prior to the captivity in Babylon. We will not do so primarily from the perspective of sophisticated biblical, historical, or literary scholarship; I am not a trained theologian, historian, or literary specialist. All such perspectives are valuable and important, and they have illumined my own understanding and writing. Indeed scholars have every good reason to ask questions about the biblical text and context. I understand my task, however, to be this: to listen with you to the biblical narrative of Jeremiah to hear what God seemed to be saying then as well as what God seems to be saying now.

While such listening may seem simple in contrast to the scholarly work described above, it is for many of us the one activity that we most often avoid in the postmodern world: listening for God's words in the reality of our everyday lives and looking for God's signs and guideposts in the moments of our days. This kind of listening is not primarily for experts and professionals, though certainly they may engage in it also. Rather this listening is best done by those of us who are still children or would like to be children, hoping beyond hope that like saints before us we have found our way into God's eternal kingdom.

Frederick Buechner, a Presbyterian preacher and writer, yearns for such childlike ears:

> When you are young, I think, your hearing is in some ways better than it is ever going to be again. You hear better than most people the voices that call to you. . . . When you are young, before you accumulate responsibilities, you are freer than most people to choose among all the voices and to answer the one that speaks most powerfully to who you are and what you really want to do with your life. But the danger is that there are so many voices. . . . The danger is that you will not listen to the voice that speaks to you. . . . To Isaiah, the voice said, "Go," and for each of us there are many voices that say it, but the question is which one will we obey.[1]

This approach is the same one that a modern prophet and theologian of the last thirty years, Walter Brueggemann, has taken in listening to Jeremiah for what God "meant" and what God "means."[2] As one of the leading Old Testament theologians in North America, Brueggemann has consistently utilized the book of Jeremiah to speak boldly and clearly to the contemporary church in the United States. For Brueggemann, only the biblical narrative offers humanity any hope of having anything to say that transforms the present and prophesies a new future.[3] Brueggemann is never content to be only a theologian. He always strives to place the biblical narrative within contemporary reality and vice versa, to trace the "dynamic equivalent" between Israel then and the church now.[4]

Despite his perspective as a theologian, Brueggemann himself suggests that scholarly views of the book of Jeremiah do not much matter. The book, he says, belongs to "the synagogue and the church," as communities that "expect to be addressed in dangerous and unsettling ways by the holiness that sounds there."[5] It belongs to ordinary human beings trying to find their way in the midst of disruption and crisis beyond their imagination. Jeremiah speaks directly to individuals caught in change that is unpredictable rather than linear and that comes from nowhere to surprise, challenge, threaten, and endanger.

This was exactly the context in which Jeremiah and the people of God found themselves in the years leading up to and culminating in the captivity of Babylon. The church today faces similar disruption and crisis that we have not yet begun to understand or accept in the same way that Jeremiah was willing to embrace the destruction of Jerusalem and the temple. In a world that now has little space for organized religion, in which many persons are no longer biblically literate, where denominations matter little to church members, and where members themselves look increasingly like their society and culture, our resistance to accepting the disruption and crisis of our own "Jerusalem" may prevent us also from imagining what God is doing now and in the future.

Time and Place

The book of Jeremiah covers six decades, from 640 to 580 BC. It ends with the captivity of Jerusalem and the destruction of the temple in 587 by King Nebuchadnezzar of Babylon. Some argue that this is the dominant event of the Old Testament. Shortly after 587, Jeremiah is exiled to Egypt, where he dies. During his lifetime, the inconceivable reality that he had prophesied came to pass. Yahweh brought about the termination of the kingly Davidic line. Masses of Judah's citizens were deported to Babylon, and the temple lay fallen—one stone upon another. The identity of Yahweh and of Yahweh's people seemed nearly annihilated.

This, however, was at the end of Jeremiah's career, one that began as early as 626 BC. At the time of Jeremiah's call by God, things did not look quite so bleak. Josiah was king (639-609), and he initiated a spiritual renewal in Judah when the law scroll was discovered in the temple. In doing so, he reacted against the pagan ways of his father, Amon, and grandfather Manasseh. Manasseh in particular had undone the spiritual reconstruction and renewal of kings before him, reintroducing Baal worship, using divination, and eventually sacrificing his own son. During Josiah's reign, Assyria, the enemy to the north, was seriously weakened, and Josiah was able to enlarge Judah's boundaries.

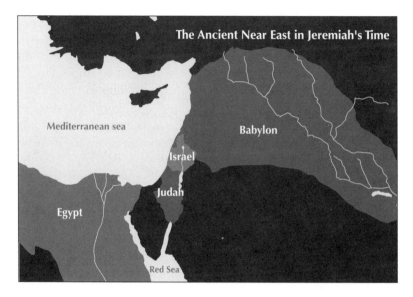

Since David's reign, Judah had been locked in a spiritual struggle of epic proportions, sometimes acknowledging God in repentance, at other times explicitly revolting against Yahweh's plans and purposes. By Jeremiah's time, the golden years of David's and Solomon's reigns sounded like fairy tales compared to the tragic stories of the kings that followed them—righteous kings followed by wicked and wicked followed by righteous—none of whom managed much of a happily ever after. Over time, the cycle of faithfulness followed by disobedience began to move both Judah and Israel toward the inevitable destruction that Jeremiah so clearly saw coming. Increasingly during the seventh and sixth centuries, foreign powers began to put pressure on Judah from both the south and the north.

A Timeline of Jeremiah's Life

Year	Event
640	Josiah begins to rule (640-609)
627	Jeremiah is called to be prophet
621	Josiah repairs the temple and the scroll is discovered
609	Josiah dies in battle with Pharaoh Neco of Egypt
605	Nebuchadnezzar becomes ruler of Babylon
604	King Jehoiakim burns Jeremiah's scroll
598/597	Babylon's armies besiege Jerusalem
597	Jehoiachin and others deported to Babylon
587	Jerusalem falls to Babylon and exiles are deported
585(?)	Jeremiah goes to Egypt

Josiah's death in 609 at the battle of Megiddo against the Egyptian king Neco accelerated the beginning of Judah's final descent toward judgment. After Josiah, Judah struggled between the dual pressures of Egypt to the south and Babylon to the north. Josiah's son, Jehoahaz, reigned only three months before he was dethroned by Egypt. The king of Egypt replaced Jehoahaz with his brother Eliakim, changing his name to Jehoiakim. Jehoiakim reigned eleven years before Nebuchadnezzar entered Jerusalem, taking the king off to Babylon along with articles from the temple. Jehoiakim was replaced by his son Jehoachin, who reigned just over three months before Nebuchadnezzar recalled him to Babylon, appointing Jehoachin's uncle Zedekiah king of Judah. But Zedekiah, going against Jeremiah's seemingly unreasonable warnings to cooperate with Nebuchadnezzar, rebelled. In response, Nebuchadnezzar destroyed Jerusalem, set fire to the temple, and carried off its citizens. Then, after years of unfaithfulness and disobedience, the "land enjoyed its sabbath rests" (2 Chronicles 36:21).

Elmer Martens, Mennonite Brethren theologian, summed up this period:

> For Judah, the turn of the century was clearly a time of transition marked by storm and stress. Judah had five different kings in its last two decades, few of them God-fearing. The prophets presented a false message, the priests were corrupt,

the scribes wrote with a "lying pen." Jeremiah . . . tried in vain to bring a spiritually wayward people back to God. He failed; they did not respond.[6]

It is within such a time of change—disruptive, unpredictable, and surprising—that Jeremiah wrote, and it is within our similar context of change that Jeremiah speaks to us still. But what exactly did—and does—the prophet have to say?

The Message

Nearly all scholars and theologians agree that two major themes dominate the book of Jeremiah: the judgment of God and the deliverance by God.[7] Most of the book's propositions can be located in one of these two themes. And of course, this is true not only for God's people during Jeremiah's time, but also for God's people today, who though living after the death and resurrection of Jesus Christ are in so many ways caught between the judgment of God and God's deliverance.

The story of God's people in the book of Jeremiah summarizes the story of God's people through all times and in all places and is characterized by five major actions:

1. God makes a covenant,
2. the people are unfaithful,
3. a prophet of God responds and imagines an inconceivable future of destruction and restoration,
4. God judges the people, and
5. God delivers.[8]

The Prophet

Jeremiah was a radical voice for God. His messages were rarely received, in large part because God's people could not fit their minds around God's imagination. So who was Jeremiah?

A *futurist*. Throughout the book, Jeremiah uses powerful poetic images to imagine a new future for Jerusalem and God's people. Like Ezekiel and Isaiah, Jeremiah stepped outside of the past to imagine what God was going to do next. Prophets and poets of Israel, until this moment in their history, had always imagined a future embedded in the old traditions and connected to the temple, where Yahweh's presence dwelt. But Jeremiah, foreseeing the destruction of Jerusalem and the temple, was free to move beyond these old traditions and realities.

Jeremiah rejected the prevailing idea that the temple could never be destroyed and God's people exiled. And in proclaiming Jerusalem's demise, he was given by God a new hope and future. Jeremiah did not have spiritual amnesia in which he forgot who God was. He simply saw new realities that others had difficulty imagining because they clung to what was already in God's past. Jeremiah was able to see the big picture of what God was up to in the world and among God's people. This perspective allowed Jeremiah to receive God's words of judgment and destruction more readily. Jeremiah's deep faith in Yahweh's love allowed the prophet to move beyond Yahweh's judgment.[9]

Martens says the book of Jeremiah is

> a miniature of the entire Old Testament, for it depicts the alienation of people from God, God's unceasing attempts to bring them back to himself, God's judgment on the evil through exile, the delights of restoration, and his actions not only on behalf of the people of Israel but for the benefit of the world of nations.[10]

A time keeper. "A prophet," says Abraham Heschel, "knows what time it is."[11] Jeremiah understood the time, and out of that understanding faithfully prophesied all that God laid upon his heart. Living according to Yahweh's time kept him detached from his culture and people. This detachment allowed him a more valid analysis of reality. From the perspective of an outsider, Jeremiah "X-rayed the culture so that all could see the falsehoods, the insincerities, the adulteries, both physical and spiritual, the violence . . . all of which had become part of the social fabric and were regarded by the populace as normal."[12] If we are going to see the world around us with new eyes we must be willing to get distance from our lives and experiences. If we are going to see beyond the present into God's future we must get outside our own sense of time and place. Jeremiah's ability and willingness to stand on the margins and to reference himself by God's time lent him the ability to see and articulate what God was up to in the world.

Brueggemann suggests that the book of Jeremiah is particularly useful both for addressing the "immense problems of biblical faith" and for engaging that faith in contemporary circumstances.[13] In this way, the book of Jeremiah—like all of Scripture—is both historical and ahistorical. It lies within an historical timeline that sometimes can be more or less discovered. But it also lies within God's timeless and eternal timeline, in which chronology gets lost and sometimes becomes irrelevant. In this way, the stories of then are timeless in their application to the stories of now.

A social analyst. In describing prophets as history makers, Brueggemann argues that they are always folks who engage in "serious, discerning social analysis and [are] social critics."[14] That is, prophets are those who simply state the truth about the world as they see it, even when such truth is resisted and rejected by others. Jeremiah, says Brueggemann, "made a decision about where the historical process was moving, and he is uncompromising in his conviction that the historical process is moving toward Babylon."[15] In reading his society and culture through Yahweh's eyes and from outside of the religious and political centers of power, Jeremiah understood where history was going, unlike the other prophets of his day.

An activist. Jeremiah's insights and obedience to God demanded that he do more than observe. He had to act. Doing so, he "moved into the crowds, challenged their falsely based security, their double-think, their manipulative ways, their god-substitutes. He became an activist confronting his peers." As both observer and activist, Jeremiah "holds a mirror to God's people today, inviting them to stand back and see their society as God sees it, but also to plunge into it to work for repentance and change."[16] Jeremiah not only spoke prophetically for the truth, but also acted prophetically on behalf of the truth.

A blasphemer. Jeremiah's message was audacious, ridiculous, and even blasphemous. Placing ourselves in the ears of his listeners, it is easy to understand why they put him in stocks, threw him in a cistern, and threatened to kill him on numerous occasions. Jeremiah's message declared that Yahweh had plans to destroy both Jerusalem (the holy city) and the temple (the most holy place). In addition, he argued that King Zedekiah should ally himself with "God's anointed," King Nebuchadnezzar of Babylon, who had already once raided the temple and was poised on the border to do so again.

It is understandable that the people would choose not to believe Jeremiah; his words to their ears were blasphemous. He not only seemed to be prophesying their own destruction, but also the destruction of their God. Despite the fact that Jeremiah's devastating message contained a silver lining that promised God's deliverance after the judgment, the people could not believe that Yahweh would bring judgment on Yahweh. But this is exactly what Jeremiah appeared to be saying. And in some respects, they were exactly right. Because of their idolatry, God was willing to destroy all that Israel and Judah considered most sacred and most central to their religious identity. For the sacredness of their religious places, practices, and identity had become more important to them than their God.

Jeremiah's message of "God's judgment on God" would later be fulfilled in the coming of Jesus Christ, God incarnate, who finally bore the full brunt of all sin, evil and darkness on behalf of and for the sake of the world that God "so loved." The Suffering Servant willingly was "pierced for our transgressions" and "crushed for our iniquities" (Isaiah 53:5) in order that we might experience the shalom of the kingdom. In the end and for our sake, God did bring judgment on God!

Conclusion

With the words of God's threats burning deep within him, Jeremiah alternated between praising God and cursing the day he was born. But in the end, he did and said whatever God commanded him. And this challenge remains for you and me today, regardless of the realities in which we find ourselves, regardless of the words that God has laid on our tongues. Will we be faithful? Will we be bold enough to declare the truth about ourselves and our own sin and failure? If not, it is unlikely we will be given God's imagination to see the future that God has planned. But if we willingly confess our idolatrous attachments to a past that God has moved beyond, we will, like Jeremiah, receive minds to see and words to speak the truth of the new heaven and new earth that Yahweh has planned for those who love him.

Some will argue that the death and resurrection of Christ have eliminated any message of judgment like that preached by Jeremiah and that in an age of grace, judgment has no relevance. Along with the myriad of voices I referred to in chapter one, I think that the reality of the church today already reflects God's judgment. I believe that the North American church is reaping a harvest of apathy, disobedience, and idolatry and will be saved only by God's grace manifested in judgment. But the good news, as in Jeremiah's day, is that God's judgment is only the preface to God's kingdom and to God's reign—a reign initiated in the coming of Jesus Christ nearly two millennia ago and put into motion by the outpouring of God's Spirit at Pentecost.

The remainder of this book will continue to address the relevance of Jeremiah's message to our lives today. I have tried to indicate that I believe most of the struggles of God's people in Jeremiah's time are still the struggles of God's people. Forsaking Yahweh for the attachments of this world, abandoning the poor, creating unholy alliances, compromising the truth of God—all of these were sins of God's people then and I believe are sins of God's people today. The church in North America also faces disruption similar to that faced by God's people in the sixth century before Christ. We have the choice to live in denial of that reality, to try to recover a past that is unrecoverable, or to embrace the disruption we face and to follow God's Spirit into God's future.

3

God's People Now

Then all the army officers . . . and all the people from the least to the greatest approached Jeremiah the prophet and said to him, "Please hear our petition and pray to the LORD your God for this entire remnant. . . . Pray that the LORD your God will tell us where we should go and what we should do. . . . Whether it is favorable or unfavorable, we will obey the LORD our God. . . .

Ten days later the word of the LORD came to Jeremiah. So he called together . . . all the people from the least to the greatest. He said to them, "This is what the LORD, the God of Israel . . . says: "If you stay in this land, I will build you up and not tear you down; I will plant you and not uproot you, for I am grieved over the disaster I have inflicted. . . .

"However, if you say, 'We will not stay in this land,' and so disobey the LORD your God, and if you say, 'No, we will go and live in Egypt, where we will not see war . . . or be hungry for bread . . . then the sword you fear will overtake you there, and the famine you dread will follow you into Egypt, and there you will die. . . . "

When Jeremiah finished telling the people all the words of the LORD their God—everything the LORD had sent him to tell them . . . all the arrogant men said to Jeremiah, "You are lying! The LORD our God has not sent you to say, 'You must not go to Egypt to settle there.' So . . . all the people disobeyed the LORD's command to stay in the land of Judah. . . . Instead . . . they entered Egypt in disobedience to the LORD."

—Jeremiah 42:1-3, 6-10, 13-14, 16; 43:1-2, 4-5, 7

While God brought the judgment prophesied by Jeremiah, it was not without compassion, both for those who were exiled and for those who remained in Judah. Many of the exiles prospered in Babylon and a remnant was permitted to live in Judah and to harvest the fruit of its land. They became afraid, however, and made plans to flee to Egypt. But as they began their journey, they stopped to ask Jeremiah for a word from God about whether they should continue. God's people assured Jeremiah that they would obey the Lord's direction. When Jeremiah returned with God's response— an unequivocal rejection of their travel plans—they promptly went to Egypt anyway.

Like the people of God in Jeremiah's day, the church in North America today faces massive change, upheaval, and disruption. This is true for all Christian traditions—Roman Catholic, Protestant, evangelical, mainline, and Anabaptist. The findings of Mennonite Member Profile 2006 reinforce this reality. When we begin to understand how much has changed in the church, the temptation for many of us is to live in denial of the changes or to try to "default" back to the church we used to know. In fact, many of our conflicts—from styles of worship to women in leadership to membership guidelines—reflect in part the tension between what some believe God did in the past and what others understand God to be doing today. One respondent in Mennonite Member Profile 2006 reflected well the feelings of disruption, but also a willingness to embrace such disruption:

> Though I would not trade Mennonites, I think we need to start seeing outside the box. Mennonite is no longer white and European or four-part harmony. Being Mennonite is having color, sounds and smells that make us neither. Let's embrace with open arms the changes. Let's focus more on being global, missional peacemakers, servants, humble, open, understanding and welcoming inside and OUTSIDE rural areas.

The book of Acts shows us that God's Spirit, as in the day of Jeremiah, delights in disrupting the stability and comfort of our realities, particularly of our religious and spiritual realities. Peter faced the challenge of the Holy Spirit's disruptive activity in Acts 10, when the Spirit sent him to the house of the Gentile Cornelius. While visiting with Cornelius and his family, the Holy Spirit was poured out upon them. While Peter willingly baptized these new

Gentile converts, Paul later confronts him for "defaulting" back to his earlier practice of requiring Gentile Christians to follow Jewish customs (see Galatians 2).

I believe that the disruption currently being felt within the church, including among Mennonites, has been initiated by God's Spirit to move us out of quiet, comfortable lifestyles, structures, and traditions and into a world in desperate need of the news of Jesus Christ. Our temptation, like Peter's, is to "default" back into our previous patterns of doing church and to deny the reality that is all around us.

I suspect that part of the disruption of the church is God's judgment for our failures to be faithful followers of Jesus Christ. But I also believe that what we are experiencing is also God's sovereign movement to prepare us to receive the kingdom and God's reign. Regardless of the reason, the reality is clear. Much has changed and in my mind there is little value in going back. Like the saints in Hebrews 11 who rejected any "opportunity to return," those with eyes and hearts of faith must embrace an unknown future, assured that following the winds of God's Spirit, though unpredictable, is a much safer bet than efforts to backtrack, looking for a path that is disappearing even as we weep.

The Location of Mennonites

This chapter begins to tell the story of God's people who, in one way or another, are connected to Mennonite Church USA and who are represented by the respondents of Mennonite Member Profile 2006. It begins the journey of looking for some road signs and guideposts that mark the social, spiritual, economic, and political location of Mennonites today, asking questions such as these: Just where are God's people today? Are we living in the land of God's promise? Are we in exile? Are we on our way back to Egypt? Do we know where we are? This chapter creates a foundation for a greater understanding of the sociological and spiritual realities that we will consider in future chapters.

In this chapter, I will stay fairly close to what sociologists often call demographic information, such as income, occupation, race and ethnicity, education, gender, marital status, and more. Demographic questions of "social location" often help to explain other variables that we will consider in later chapters, such as how often we attend church, what we believe about the Bible, how regularly we pray, and whether we talk to our neighbors about Jesus.

It is a basic sociological assumption that social position and location (sometimes referred to as our social status) shape how we see the world, how we see the church, and how we see and experience God. Even the Scripture affirms this; otherwise Jesus would not have been so critical of those with power in the middle of society and so compassionate with those on the margins. Jesus understood the power of social location, which is why he so often sided with children and those who were down and out. Jesus understood that where we are in society—often dictated by our education, occupation, and wealth—shapes who we think we are and how we relate to one another and to God. So while these questions of income, race and ethnicity, education, and so on may seem less interesting than questions about a member's willingness to go to war or the proportion of Mennonites who own hand guns or attitudes about homosexuality, where we stand socially in society has an effect on what we believe and how we practice our faith.

This is not to say that God's Spirit is bound by demographic characteristics; clearly the Spirit is not. Throughout history, God has used persons of all races, ethnicities, income, and education to do God's will and purposes. The people of Judah illustrate this; both kings and the poor chose to disobey God. In the end, God is looking for obedient and faithful hearts, regardless of where and who we are. And yet, sociological realities do matter: we live in a social world and we are shaped by that world in powerful ways.

Declines in Denominational Membership

Mennonite Church USA is composed of two former denominations that merged in 2002: the General Conference Mennonite Church and the (Old) Mennonite Church. General Conference Mennonites had historic Dutch/Russian and Canadian origins before settling in the United States, while (Old) Mennonite Church members had Swiss/German origins. In 1972, the time of the first member profile, these two denominations together had 123,847 members in the United States. By 1989, the year of the second profile, they had grown to 130,329 members.[1] Today Mennonite Church USA has 16% fewer members (109,000) than did these two denominations in 1989.[2]

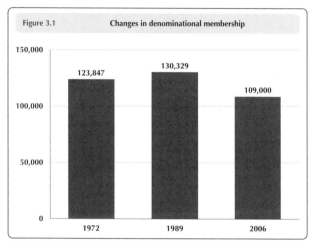

Figure 3.1 — Changes in denominational membership

As the number of members of Mennonite Church USA declines, the denomination's national and global share among Anabaptists is also diminishing. In 1989, members of the (Old) Mennonite Church and General Conference of Mennonites represented about 15% of the global population of Anabaptists (Mennonites and Brethren in Christ) and 49% of U.S. Anabaptists. Today members of Mennonite Church USA represent just 7% of global Anabaptists and 22% of all Mennonites and Brethren in Christ in the United States.[3]

Characteristics of Congregations

Geographic location. Members of Mennonite Church USA are distributed across the United States, but the vast majority live east of the Mississippi River. Pennsylvania leads all other states with 263 Mennonite congregations (27% of the denomination).

Rounding out the top five states are Ohio with 80 congregations (8% of the denomination), Indiana with 63 congregations (7% of the denomination), Illinois with 50 congregations (5% of the denomination), and Kansas with 49 congregations (5% of the denomination).

The congregations of Mennonite Church USA are distributed across twenty-one area conferences. Lancaster Mennonite Conference is the largest of these, with nearly 20% of all congregations in the denomination. Indiana-Michigan is second largest with 9% of the denomination's congregations, followed by Ohio (8%) and Virginia (7%).

Size. Mennonite congregations range in size from house churches with just a few members to congregations of more than two thousand. One-third (34%) of Mennonite congregations have fewer than fifty members, 62% have fewer than one hundred members, and three-quarters of Mennonite congregations have less than one hundred and fifty members. Seventeen percent have memberships of two hundred or more. The median congregational size is seventy-two members. The largest congregation, Calvary Community Church, in Hampton, Virginia, is home to 2,235 members.

The size of Mennonite congregations is slightly larger than the U.S. national average, where 71% of religious congregations have

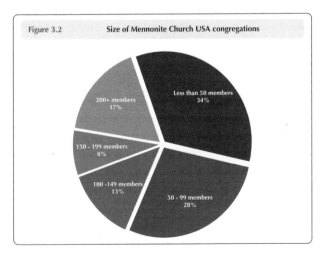

Figure 3.2   Size of Mennonite Church USA congregations

fewer than one hundred adult participants and the median attendance is fifty participating adults.[4]

Regional differences. Mennonites in our sample were distributed across the four regions of the United States as follows: 32% in the East, 50% in the Midwest, 6% in the West, and 12% in the South.[5] Members of Mennonite Church USA differ substantially from one another according to the region where they live. Here are some examples of these differences.

- Mennonites in the West are more likely to have come from non-Mennonite denominations—38% baptized in non-Mennonite congregations compared to 23% in the East and South, and 22% in the Midwest.
- Mennonites in the Midwest are most likely to be "cradle" Mennonites, with 72% having parents who were both Mennonite.
- Mennonites in the South are less mobile than other Mennonites, with 40% living in the same community for thirty years or more.
- Mennonites in the East are most rural—only 13% live in cities of fifty thousand or more residents, compared to 71% in the West.
- Mennonites in the East have the lowest levels of education, with 26% of members who have a college degree, compared to 43-47% in all other regions.

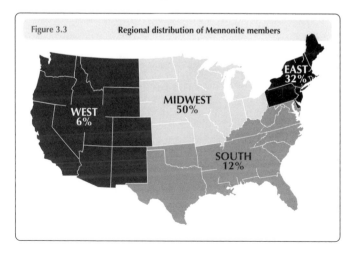

Figure 3.3   Regional distribution of Mennonite members

EAST 32%

MIDWEST 50%

WEST 6%

SOUTH 12%

Increase in Racial/Ethnic Members

The growth of Racial/Ethnic congregations is changing the face of Mennonite Church USA. Nearly 18% of Mennonite congregations are Racial/Ethnic. With more than twelve thousand members, these congregations compose 11% of the denomination's membership. In 1991, 6% of members in the (Old) Mennonite Church were Racial/Ethnic.[6] Today, perhaps as many as 15% of the denomination's members are Racial/Ethnic, including Racial/Ethnic members who attend predominantly white Mennonite congregations. In the past five years, one out of every four (25%) new members was Racial/Ethnic, compared to 6% among those who entered the denomination six or more years ago.

The largest proportion of Racial/Ethnic congregations are Latino/Hispanic (46%), followed by African-American (35%), Asian (11%), and Native American (8%). African-Americans hold the largest membership block with 52% of Racial/Ethnic members in the denomination (one-third of these attend a single congregation—Calvary Community Church, Virginia), followed by Latino/Hispanic members (35%), Asian members (9%), and Native American members (4%). Of the six congregations in Mennonite Church USA with one thousand members or more, three are Racial/Ethnic: Sonida de

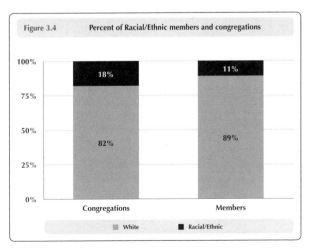

Figure 3.4   Percent of Racial/Ethnic members and congregations

Alabanza and Centro Cristiano Vida Abundante in Chicago (both Latino/Hispanic) and Calvary Community Church in Hampton, Virginia, (African-American).

Fifty-five percent of the Racial/Ethnic members in our sample were born outside the United States, including 97% of Asians, 80% of Latino/Hispanics, and 17% of African-Americans. Among Latino/Hispanic members from outside the United States, 48% migrated from Mexico, 18% from Puerto Rico, and the remainder from other countries. Among Asians, 38% migrated from Indonesia, 25% from Vietnam, and the remainder from elsewhere. In reporting the national origin of their ancestors, 71% of white Mennonites identified their origins as Swiss/German and 13% as Dutch/ Russian.

The geographic centers for Mennonite Racial/Ethnic members are different from those in the denomination as a whole. While Pennsylvania (28 Racial/Ethnic congregations) and Illinois (14) remain in the top five states with Racial/Ethnic congregations, they are joined by California (23), Texas (15), and New York (12). As the number of Racial/Ethnic congregations grows, it will mean a geographic shift in Mennonite population from East to South and West, as well as a residential shift from rural (Elkhart, Indiana; Lancaster, Pennsylvania; Newton, Kansas) to urban areas including Philadelphia, New York City, Chicago, Dallas, Miami, and Los Angeles.

Growth of Members from Other Denominations

A major shift among Mennonites over the past three decades has been the increase in members from other denominations. This change is seen at several different levels.

First, the percentage of "non-cradle" Mennonites—neither parent being Mennonite—rose from 17% to 26% between 1972 and 1989, but has not changed since 1989.

Second, the percentage of all Mennonites who have been members in another denomination at some point in their lives, including those who were originally members of a Mennonite congregation, has increased from 14% in 1972 to 23% in 1989 to 30% today. Of these members in 2006, 39% came from conservative Protestant denominations (for example, Southern Baptists, Assemblies of God, or Independent) 38% from mainline Protestant denominations (such as United Methodist, Presbyterian, United Church of Christ), 12% from other Anabaptist-related churches (such as the Church of the Brethren, or Brethren in Christ), and 6% from Roman Catholicism. These members are disproportionately from mainline Protestant denominations as only 22% of Americans identify as mainline Protestant compared to 34% who identify as conservative Protestant.[7]

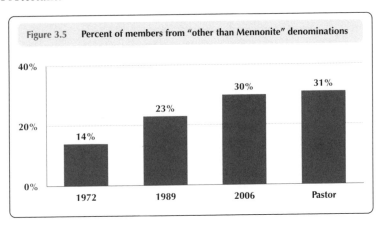

Figure 3.5   **Percent of members from "other than Mennonite" denominations**

Third, the percentage of Mennonite members who married a spouse from another denomination rose from 25% in 1972 to 39% in 1989—where it remains today.

Finally, among all Mennonites, only 2% are new believers; they did not attend church as children and were not members of another church before becoming Mennonite. Sixty-four percent are cradle Mennonites who were raised in a Mennonite home and have always been Mennonite. Thirty-four percent are transfers from other denominations, including: a) 9% who were cradle Mennonites before becoming a member of another denomination, b) 21% who did not grow up Mennonite, and c) 4% who grew up going to a non-Mennonite church but were never members elsewhere before joining a Mennonite congregation.

All of these findings suggest that the entrance of new members into Mennonite congregations has slowed since 1989, and that the proportion of new Christians is quite low within the denomination as a whole.

A Rapidly Aging Membership

The mean age of Mennonites today is 54, five years older than in 1989.[8] While the aging of Mennonite Church USA parallels national and global trends, the pace of the aging is more extreme than among other religious denominations in the United States. In 1972, 54% of Mennonites were between the ages of 18 and 45— within childbearing age. This number declined to 45% in 1989 and is only 30% today. This change has been greater for Mennonites than even for mainline Protestant denominations, which a recent study described as "literally dying out" despite less drastic changes in their age distribution.[9] Among mainline Protestant denominations, 42% of members are under 45, compared to 52% of conservative Protestants. While 15% of Mennonites are 75 or older, only 12% of mainline Protestants and 7% of conservative Protestants are as old.

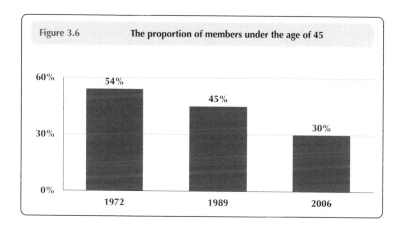

Figure 3.6   **The proportion of members under the age of 45**

While these comparisons with mainline and conservative Protestants were based on members 18 years of age or older, comparisons with Americans as a whole need to account for the fact that Mennonite Member Profile 2006 members were 18 years of age or older. To obtain a more direct comparison of Mennonites and Americans, further analysis revealed that 31% of Mennonites over the age of 20 are 65 years or older compared to only 17% of Americans who are the same age.[10]

Racial/Ethnic members are much younger than other Mennonites and add a glimmer of demographic hope to an aging church. Racial/Ethnic members are nine years younger (46 years old) on average than Anglo Mennonites (55 years old). While the percentage of white Mennonites between the ages of 18 and 45 is only 29%, 50% of Racial/Ethnic members are in this same category.

Declining family size. The changing age distribution among Mennonites and the simultaneous decline in denominational membership is likely related in part to a decline in family size among Mennonites. In 1972, women in their childbearing years (18-44) had on average 2.1 children. In 1989, women the same age had 1.7 children. Today Mennonite women average 1.4 children.

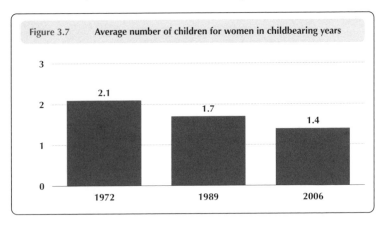

Figure 3.7   **Average number of children for women in childbearing years**

Racial/Ethnic differences exist both nationally and among Mennonites. In the United States, white women ages 15-44 have 1.9

children, African-Americans 2.0, Native Americans 1.7, Asians 1.9, and Hispanics 2.8.[11] White Mennonite women of childbearing age have 1.4 children. Racial/Ethnic Mennonite women as a group have slightly more (1.6), but there is substantial variation by Racial/Ethnic group, with African-American women averaging 2.3 children, Asian women 0.6, Native Americans 2.3, and Latino/Hispanics 2.0.

From 1972 to 1989, the decline in number of children among Mennonites was offset by the increase in non-cradle Mennonites. This increase has stagnated since 1989, however, while the fertility rate has continued to decline. Should lower birth rates persist without the substantial addition of new members who are not Mennonite, the denomination faces a bleak future. The younger age of Racial/Ethnic members, however, is a boost as are the higher fertility rates of some Racial/Ethnic groups.

Differences Between Younger and Older Members

Mennonites between the ages of 18-35 are less engaged in the church than are older members. While 86% of older members (36 years plus) consider themselves "active" members of their congregation, only 69% of younger members do so. Younger members attend church less often (68% weekly compared to 83% of older members) as well as Sunday school (39% compared to 57% of older members). In addition, fewer younger members say that their relationship with their congregation is very important to them (40% completely agreeing compared to 57% of older Mennonites).

These differences are likely related in part to the fact that younger members are more highly educated (50% with a four-year degree compared to 36% of older members), more likely to be single (37% compared to 6% of older members), and slightly more likely to live in an urban area (26% vs. 20% of older members). While younger members are as likely as older to say that their religious beliefs are important to them, they are less likely to embrace "distinct" Mennonite beliefs and also care less about denominational differences.

Increased Assimilation

In *Mennonite Mosaic*, Kauffman and Driedger found that Mennonites were becoming increasingly assimilated into the broader American culture, meaning that they were looking more and more like the rest of society in their lifestyle choices.[12] This trend has accelerated since 1989 for white Mennonites. Racial/Ethnic Mennonites, however, differ substantially from white Mennonites, being less assimilated into the larger culture.

Less rural. In 1972, 36% of Mennonites lived on a farm, compared to 26% in 1989 and 12% today. Of Mennonites today, more than 40% grew up on a farm, but of those, fewer than one-fourth (23%) remain on the farm. While twice as many Mennonites live in large cities of 250,000 or more as did in 1989, this number still accounts for less than 10% of all Mennonites. The primary residential areas that Mennonites have migrated to when leaving the farm are small and medium cities and suburbs. Racial/Ethnic members in our sample are much more urban than other Mennonites, with 39% living in cities of more than 250,000 persons.

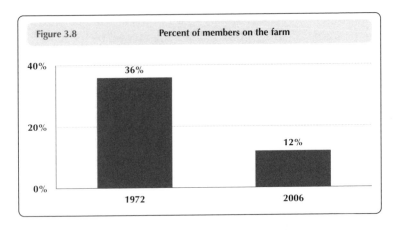

Figure 3.8   **Percent of members on the farm**

No change in mobility. Interestingly, while Mennonites are less rural and more suburban than in the past (with the exception of Racial/Ethnic members), they are no more mobile than three decades ago. The proportion of Mennonites who lived in the same community for at least twenty years was 52% in 1972 and 53% today. And those in the same community four years or less was 17% in 1972 and 16% in 2006. Among Racial/Ethnic members, however, only 30% have lived in the same community for twenty-plus years and 25% have lived in their current community for four years or less. The greater mobility of Racial/Ethnic members should not be surprising, given that more than half (55%) of these members in our sample were born outside the United States.

More professional. The proportion of Mennonites who are in business and professional occupations has risen from 25% in 1972 to 41% today, as has the percentage in technical, sales, and administrative support—from 7% to 27%. The number of service workers doubled from 3% in 1972 to 8% in 2006, while the percentage of farmers declined from 11% to 8% today. The percentage of members claiming "housewife/homemaker" as their occupation decreased from 35% in 1972 to only 7% in 2006. The major difference in occupation among Racial/Ethnic members is the fact that almost twice as many are in service occupations.

Table 3.1	Occupations of Mennonite members			
	1972	1989	2006	Racial/ Ethnic
Managerial and Professional	23	37	41	39
Technical, Sales, and Admin. Support	7	10	27	26
Service	3	4	8	15
Farming, Forest, Fishing	11	9	8	3
Precision Production, Craft, Repair	5	6	8	8
Operators, Fabricators, and Laborers	8	5	8	9
Housewife/Homemaker	35	26	7	10
Student	8	4	3	2
	Percent			

The number of Mennonites working full time declined since 1972. The number of retired members is higher today than in either of the previous studies. Today 21% report being fully retired, compared to 14% in 1989 and 5% in 1972. Racial/Ethnic members are more likely to be employed full time than Mennonites as a whole (54%) and are less likely to be retired (10%).

Higher levels of education. Mennonites are highly educated and increasingly so, with 38% (37% of women and 40% of men) having graduated from college, compared to 20% in 1972. Mennonites are also more highly educated than Americans as a whole—29% of American men have a college degree and 26% of women.[13] While 88% of Mennonite respondents have at least a high school diploma, only 52% of their fathers and 58% of their mothers graduated from high school. And only 17% of their fathers and 14% of their mothers graduated from college. While 37% of Racial/Ethnic members in our sample are college graduates, there are substantial differences in education among Racial/Ethnic groups. Fifty-six percent of Asians have a college degree, 32% of African-Americans, 21% of Latino/Hispanics, and 12% of Native Americans. Native Americans are most likely not to have completed high school at 41%, followed by Latino/Hispanics at 23%.

Mennonites are more highly educated than Protestants nationally. While 38% of Mennonites have a college degree, 30% of mainline Protestants are as equally educated, 17% of conservative Protestants, 11% of African-Americans, and 31% of Americans with no religious identity.[14] Demographic research suggests that education is closely related to the fertility rates of a group. As people become more educated, the number of children they have declines. This finding holds true for Mennonites as well. Mennonite women 18-45 years of age with a high school diploma or less have on average 1.8 children, close to the national average of 1.9. This compares with 1.5 children among Mennonite women with some college education (but not a four year degree) and 1.3 children among Mennonite women with at least a four-year college degree.

Table 3.2	Education levels of Mennonites			
	1972	1989	2006	Racial/ Ethnic
Less than high school grad	35	19	12	17
High school grad	29	30	22	16
Some college	17	20	28	30
College grad	6	11	17	17
Some grad school	4	5	6	5
Graduate degree	9	15	16	15
	Percent			

Income. The 2005 median household income of Mennonites was between $50,000 to $75,000 with 25% of members in that income bracket. Forty-seven percent had household incomes less than $50,000 while 28% had more $75,000.

Racial/Ethnic members are less affluent and more likely to experience poverty. In 2005, 18% of Racial/Ethnic households had incomes under $15,000, compared with only 6% of Anglo Mennonites. One-third of Racial/Ethnic households earned under $25,000 and nearly two-thirds less than $50,000, compared to 15% of white Mennonites who earned less than $25,000 and 45% who earned less than $50,000. Additionally, the average size of Racial/Ethnic households that earned less that $25,000 was 3.1 persons compared to 2.2 persons in other Mennonite households that earned as much. In other words, not only are Racial/Ethnic members more likely to earn less than other Mennonites, they also support more persons on that lower income. Among Americans as a whole in the year 2000, 20% earned between $50,000 and $75,000, 23% earned more, and 58% earned less.[15]

Other variables that indicate economic disparities between Racial/Ethnic Mennonites and others include:
- Sixteen percent lack healthcare insurance, compared to just 4% of white Mennonites (16% of Americans do not have health insurance).

- Sixty-five percent own their own homes, compared to 88% of white Mennonites.

Stability in Marriage and Family

Almost four-fifths (78%) of Mennonites are married, 11% are single, 7% are widowed, 2% are currently divorced, and 1% are separated or living in some other arrangement. The percentage of Mennonites who are currently divorced has increased slightly since 1972 but shows remarked stability and remains substantially lower than for Americans as a whole and among other denominations. Just over 10% of Mennonites in our sample have been divorced at some time in their lives.

Compared with other faith traditions, Mennonite families are more intact. Among conservative and mainline Protestants, 19% of respondents are currently divorced or separated, while among those with no religious affiliation, 21% are divorced or separated. Eleven percent of Mennonites in our sample were never married, compared to 16% of conservative Protestants and 17% of mainline Protestants in the United States.

A Church Disrupted: Crisis or Opportunity?

The picture that emerges of Mennonites in the United States today is dramatically different from the snapshot taken by J. Howard Kauffman and Leland Harder in 1972. What are the key findings of this chapter and their implications?

Membership decline. The number of members in Mennonite Church USA is substantially fewer than the combined memberships of the (Old) Mennonite Church and the General Conference Mennonite Church in 1972. In addition, the proportion of Mennonite Church USA members among other Anabaptists globally and in the United States is declining, a factor affected by the denomination's actual decline in membership and increases among other Anabaptists groups (Brethern in Christ, Old Order groups, and Anabaptists in the global south).

The declining number of members in Mennonite Church USA

reflects several changes. First, the baby boomers who were of child-bearing age in the first two Church Member Profiles are now out of childbearing age, lowering the proportion of members under the age of 45. Second, persons today have longer life expectancies than thirty-five years ago, contributing to the growing proportion of older persons in the church. Third, fertility rates are lower today than in the past, so fewer children are being born. Fourth, since 1989, the proportion of non-cradle Mennonites has remained the same. And as I noted earlier, only 2% of members are new believers. So while we are getting older and having fewer children, we are not growing in the number of new members from other denominations or in new Christians.

Without an increase in fertility rates among Mennonites—an unlikely event—the denomination will need to rely on the recruitment of new members simply to sustain its current levels of membership. Without such recruitment, Mennonite Church USA, like a number of other denominations in the United States, must come to grips with the fact that it will not be sustainable in the coming decades. This fact alone should motivate Mennonites to embrace a missional future. If it does not, perhaps nothing will.

Disengagement of young adults. The lower levels of involvement of Mennonite young people in congregations and in the denomination should be of concern to all of us. Sociological research shows that marrying and having children typically causes persons to return to church, and often the church of their childhood. Americans today, however, are prolonging marriage and childbearing more so than in the past. Doing so means fewer children once individuals do marry as well as a delayed return to the church. It is critical that Mennonites engage our young adults, with the denomination experiencing both overall membership decline as well as lower fertility rates. Becoming a missional church must go hand in hand with nurturing those young persons already in our churches. It would be a tragedy to missionally engage those across the street and around the world while at the same time ignoring our own children, teenagers, and young adults.

Growth in numbers of Racial/Ethnic members. Mennonite

Church USA is more racially and ethnically diverse than in the past. Racial/Ethnic members are much younger on average than Anglo members and have higher fertility rates, providing a much-needed population boost to the denomination. Unfortunately, many Anglo—that is, white—Mennonites have little awareness of the number and growth of these members. At the same time, Racial/Ethnic leaders and members feel alienated and outside of the structures of power and relationships of the church.

In visiting with Racial/Ethnic pastors over the past two years, I repeatedly heard their desire to partner with Anglo congregations in ministry. Many had painful stories of experiences where Anglo Mennonites had, unintentionally at times, failed to keep promises or to follow through on commitments. Numerous barriers confront the development of relationships among Anglo members and Racial/Ethnic members, including
- historic prejudice and discrimination in the church and in society,
- differences in language and culture,
- residential patterns in which many Racial/Ethnic members live in cities while most Anglos live in suburban and rural areas,
- economic inequalities, and
- educational differences.

My conversations and analysis over the past two years within Mennonite Church USA have convinced me that finding new and creative ways to cross racial and ethnic boundaries in the church is perhaps the most important challenge and opportunity facing the denomination. But if new patterns of relating, including the redistribution of power and resources do not develop, I suspect that some Racial/Ethnic members will leave the denomination. If they do, the church will have missed perhaps its last and best opportunity for renewal.

Regional diversity. The regional differences across Mennonite Church USA likely have been exacerbated by the merger of the two denominations—General Conference Mennonite Church and the (Old) Mennonite Church—perhaps creating greater regional diversity than existed within either former denomination. The challenges of leading and unifying a church as regionally diverse as Mennonite Church USA are many.

Becoming like the culture. Mennonites are more like the larger culture and society in the United State than in previous surveys, although differences remain between Anglos and Racial/Ethnic members in this regard. Mennonites are more educated than in the past, more professional in their occupational choices, and less rural. (These changes will be reflected upon in future chapters that address religious beliefs and practices.) While identifying more closely with the broader culture, we have an opportunity to become a more missional people, connecting to hurting persons in need of the gospel. The risk in becoming more like those around us, however, is that we will slowly forget who we are and will be co-opted by our society and culture. As Mennonites have changed demographically, we have become less active in our church participation and more shaped by the broader culture, highlighting the difficulty of being "in the world" without being "of the world."

Some will celebrate changes in the church that we have observed in this chapter and others will grieve them. Some will become anxious. Some will deny them. In fact, as I have reported findings about the denomination's membership decline and the aging of its members, persons have tended to respond in three different ways. Some challenge the data. Others argue that while the data are probably correct, the aging of Mennonites merely parallels the aging of the nation and of other denominations. Still others point out numerous reasons—and most of them correct—as to why the aging is occurring. All three types of responses are appropriate and worthwhile discussing. However, each avoids the bottom line: that without the infusion of new members into the denomination there will be no future for the church. The challenge for modern and postmodern persons is to overcome the tendency to analyze ourselves into oblivion and to get on with God's mission to the world.

While the disruption facing Mennonites in the United States is unique in some respects, it also reflects the challenges and crises that other denominations in North America are facing today. The temptation for all of us, including church leaders, is to try to manage the changes—to become history stoppers in an effort to counter the disruption we face. But we have a unique opportunity in this moment to be history makers like Jeremiah by embracing the disruption and asking the missional question: "God, what *in the world* are you doing?"

4

The Call

The word of the LORD came to me saying, "Before I formed you in the womb I knew you, before you were born I set you apart; I appointed you as a prophet to the nations."

"Ah, Sovereign LORD," I said, "I do not know how to speak; I am only a child."

But the LORD said to me, "Do not say, 'I am only a child.' You must go to everyone I send you to and say whatever I command you. . . ."

Then the LORD reached out his hand and touched my mouth and said to me, "Now, I have put my words in your mouth."

—Jeremiah 1:4-7, 9

Whenever God calls, it is always a call to go—whether across the street or around the world. And God is always calling—to Abram and Sarai living comfortably in Ur, to the seventy-two disciples sent by Jesus in Luke 10, to Saul on the road to Damascus, and to all of us living in the wake of our Lord's great commission. While this "going" may not always require a geographic change of location, it always comes with an expectation that, like Jeremiah, we will speak God's words and do everything God asks of us.

In calling Jeremiah, God commissioned him to be a spokesperson to the nations and to "everyone that I send you to." When Jeremiah stammered that he was only a child and unable to speak, Yahweh touched his mouth and put inspired words within it, words that would later predict the destruction of nearly everything that God's people believed to be sacred.

A Childlike Response

The date of Jeremiah's call by God is debated, but some scholars suggest 627 BC, during the reign of Josiah, the last righteous king of Judah. Jeremiah's responsive obedience to God's call, as compared to the more languished responses of others in Scripture was perhaps related to Jeremiah's youthfulness. He had not yet developed the kind of skepticism that some adults seem to have about God's call and the reality of God's presence. Jeremiah simply heard the Creator utter his name. And like the child Samuel centuries earlier, and like that other Child centuries later, Jeremiah's response was immediate and faithful.

While Jeremiah's gift to God was a lifetime of obedience, God's gift to him was a mouthful of fiery words that his bones could hardly contain. These words brought him ridicule, scorn, and insult, tormenting him and his listeners. And quite frankly, they torment us still—both for their promise of God's judgment because of our disobedience as well as for their assurance of a new future. If Jeremiah had ever been tempted to give himself or his parents any credit for God's call upon his life, such temptations were soon dissolved in the curses he uttered about the day of his birth and about those who had announced his coming into the world.

But why does God so often call children—Samuel, David, Mary the mother of Jesus, and the disciple John, among others? Perhaps it is because children still have an imagination to see God's reality and to believe that things can be different than they currently are. Children are resilient; though they may suffer much, they continue to trust and to believe. Children are vulnerable and dependent upon others.

When the seventy-two disciples returned to Jesus after being sent out by him to proclaim that the kingdom of God was near, Jesus looked to heaven and thanked the Father for revealing the kingdom to children and not to the "wise and learned" (Luke 10:21). For the wise and learned too often think they do not need Jesus, depending on their own tools and techniques to accomplish the kingdom's work. But Jesus' call is a simple one: "Come and follow me." And children are the ones who seem to hear that call most clearly.

An Outsider's Perspective

If being a child was a factor in why God called Jeremiah, another may have been his status as an outsider. As the son of Hilkiah the priest, Jeremiah came from a long line of outsiders, a family of priests who had been marginalized by their banishment from Jerusalem by King Solomon in 1 Kings 2.[1] This exile from the geographic center of God's holiness made Jeremiah an outsider to the royal kings and the religious leaders to whom God sent him. It is a common sociological assumption that social outsiders—those without power, wealth, prestige and status—are able to see and hear social realities to which social insiders are blind and deaf. There is much in Scripture to support this assumption, including Jesus' continuous railing against the spiritual elites and history stoppers of his day. Too often, for those on the inside, the call and message of God are perceived as a threat to hard-earned status and prestige. It was those on the margins during Jesus' ministry—women, tax collectors, prostitutes, and the poor—who most warmly embraced their Lord and who were most warmly embraced by him.

But though an outsider, Jeremiah was in a unique position. As the child of a priestly family, he was taught and trained in the teachings of Yahweh while growing up. So if Jeremiah's marginality gave him a clearer view of both royalty and the priesthood that is often hidden from those in the centers of power, his knowledge of God was drawn from the generations of faithful priests who had gone before him. God's words through Jeremiah were fueled by the perspective of an outsider and by the faithfulness of an insider.

Pitted Against the World

During the decades that Jeremiah prophesied, God gave him messages for both Judah and Israel as well as the surrounding nations of Egypt, Moab, and Babylon. More than any other Old Testament prophet, Jeremiah was "pitted against the whole world."[2] Kings, prophets, priests, and ordinary people despised him. He was the subject of an assassination attempt, threatened with lynching, imprisoned, and thrown in a cistern to die. Both prophets and priests opposed him; Hananiah the prophet broke a wooden yoke over Jeremiah's neck and Pashur the priest threw him in prison.

It is hard to fathom the courage that Jeremiah needed in order to persevere. The memory of his calling by Yahweh—of being given the words of God by God's own hand—undoubtedly gave him strength for the task. The fact that some form of the phrase "Thus says the Lord" appears 150 times in the book of Jeremiah suggests that the prophet could not bear to lose sight of the source of his words—that his was a divine call. Had he forgotten his calling, he might have quickly surrendered to the opposition. But Jeremiah continued to provide road signs and guideposts for God's people, addressing their sin, predicting God's judgment, and all the while imagining a new and prosperous future.

Emotional and Transparent

Jeremiah is more reflective and transparent than any other Old Testament prophet. He freely describes the deep personal pain and heartache caused by obedience to God's call. Attacked by kings, prophets, priests, and common people, let down by his parents simply because they brought him into the world, and seemingly abandoned by his Creator, the tormenting words of God simply would not go away. They lay deep within his soul. His skin and bones could not contain them. Like a geyser, they had to come out. Because the fiery words of God threatened to annihilate Jeremiah and the heavy words of God to suffocate him, he had to release them. And yet doing so always got him into trouble—with the kings of Judah, with the false prophets, and with just about everybody else. His only recourse was to curse the day he was born as well as those who had celebrated that day—certainly no one had celebrated much about him since!

The Calling of Mennonites

Jeremiah's experience raises interesting questions for the people of God today. To what extent do we see ourselves as called by

God—as individuals, as congregations, and as a denomination? Have we been obedient in responding to God's call—in our homes, across the street, and around the world? What are the implications of our faithfulness or lack of faithfulness in answering God's call?

In coming to identify our missional vocation or calling—as individuals, congregations, and a denomination—we must recognize that all of us are called and sent by God to give witness to the good news of salvation in Jesus Christ. Every congregation and denomination that exists today does so because God continues to have plans and purposes for them—to be the healing and saving presence of Christ to the world. This is the first and primary call of God's people.

It would be easy to blame the membership decline in Mennonite Church USA on a loss of evangelistic fervor. Like others who have studied the North American church, however, I conclude that a primary reason for our decline is not simply less commitment to evangelism and outreach (though there is evidence of this too), but rather the demographic changes of lower fertility rates, the aging of the baby boomers, and longer life expectancies. In fact, I would argue that Mennonites in the United States have lived for centuries without much commitment to being evangelistic—at least in our local communities. Our churches remained full because we had large families. But as fertility rates have declined, it is apparent that we were never doing a very good job of reaching the world right around us for Christ, despite effective global mission efforts. Many of those who remain in our congregations are descendants of those who were in the pews several generations ago; and there are fewer of them today than in the past.

Thus, this chapter addresses the challenges that Mennonite members face in hearing and responding to God's call as individuals, congregations, and a denomination.

Belief, but Little Action

Mennonite members consistently agreed that church planting and evangelism should be priorities of the denomination, and 88% believe that "Christians should do all they can to convert all nonbelievers to Christ." Personal efforts to evangelize, however, are not consistent with the priority members believe evangelism should have in the denomination. One-third of Mennonites have never invited a non-Christian to attend a service or activity at their church, and only 13% do as frequently as once a month or more. Just over half (58%) have ever tried "to convert others to faith in Christ" and only 18% do so on a regular basis (monthly or more).

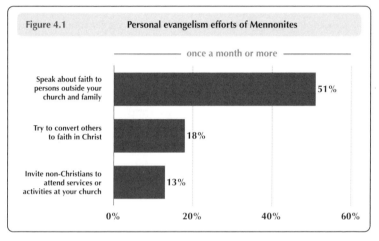

Figure 4.1   Personal evangelism efforts of Mennonites

once a month or more

Speak about faith to persons outside your church and family — 51%

Try to convert others to faith in Christ — 18%

Invite non-Christians to attend services or activities at your church — 13%

0%   20%   40%   60%

Evangelism efforts appear to have declined over three decades. In 1972, 16% of members had never invited a non-Christian to church (compared to 33% in 2006). Seventy-seven percent had tried to lead someone to faith (compared to 58% in 2006) in Christ.

Mennonite evangelistic efforts are lower than for conservative Protestants in the United States, among whom 71% say they have tried to encourage someone to believe in Jesus Christ or to accept Christ as their Savior. Forty-three percent of mainline Protestants say they have done so.[3]

Racial/Ethnic Mennonites are more evangelistic than other Mennonites. Eighty percent have tried to convert someone to Christ at some point in their lives and 48% do so at least monthly. Eighty-seven percent of Racial/Ethnic members have invited non-Christians to church and 45% do so frequently. Sixty-seven percent regularly speak to others about their faith, compared to 51% of other Mennonites.

Not surprisingly, new members to Mennonite congregations are also more evangelistic than long-time members. Of members who joined a Mennonite church within the past five years, 27% regularly try to convert others to faith in Christ (monthly or more) and 23% invite non-Christians to their church.

So while Mennonites believe that the denomination and its agencies should be committed to evangelism and outreach, they seem less willing than in the past to personally engage others with the Gospel.

For pastors and missionaries only. The failure of many of us to obey God's call may lie in an assumption that such a call is primarily for certain "special" people—for pastors, missionaries, and other church leaders. Findings from Mennonite Member Profile 2006 suggest that Mennonite church members resist seeing themselves as "ministers," and efforts by pastors to challenge this notion receive little support. Ministry, including evangelism and outreach, too often remain the place of those who have been "credentialed" for that task.

While assigning greater spiritual and social authority to pastors, credentialing also sends an implicit message to members that they are either incapable of or not needed for real ministry. In this way, the local congregation becomes a place that members attend in order to be ministered to rather than a place to be equipped for ministry in the coming week. Any church that is going to effectively share Christ with its local community must have members—and not just the pastor(s)—who understand that it is their responsibility to do so. Churches that fail to create "ministers" of members will never develop their missional calling to share Christ in word and deed with their neighbors. And frankly, the profile findings suggest little future for a church that does not become missional—committed above all else to sharing Christ in word and deed with the world around it.

Tensions often develop between the efforts of pastors to equip and prepare members for ministry and members who seem unwilling to accept that ministry is for them. When pastors in Mennonite Member Profile 2006 were given a list of thirteen leadership tasks and asked to indicate those most important to them, "equipping the members for ministry" was just below preaching (48%) and shaping the congregation's vision (42%), with 41% of pastors identifying this as one of their top priorities. When members were given the same question about pastor priorities, 46% identified preaching and 32% identified pastoral care as the two most important, with only 17% marking "equipping members for ministry."

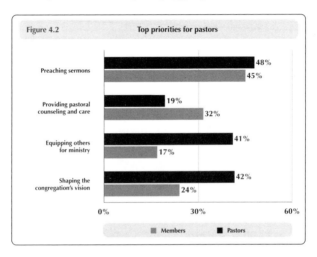

Figure 4.2 — Top priorities for pastors

While pastors believe that equipping members to minister should be one of their top priorities, it is not nearly as important to members. Members generally want their pastors to preach and provide care—in other words, to minister to them. Missional churches, however, will prepare all members to "minister" Christ's healing and hope to the world.

Gathered—not sent. The unwillingness or inability to accept the view that all Christians are ministers creates an implicit—and sometimes explicit—assumption that church is a place for gathering one day a week rather than a place from which to be sent as ministers into the world. In truly missional congregations, more ministry happens outside the walls of the church building during the week than within them on Sunday morning. As Christians, we too often see ourselves as the church when we are gathered on Sunday morning but not when we are sent by Jesus into the world throughout the week.

If members are going to be faithful to God's call, it is going to require them to be more receptive to being in the role of ministering, not only to one another, but also to those outside the church. As Mennonites whose ancestors rediscovered the priesthood of all believers, we have too often lapsed into an understanding of the priesthood that is more like that of the faith traditions we abandoned during the Reformation.

Missional churches understand that the church is the product of God's mission to the world, and that the mission always takes priority over the church, for without mission there would be no church. Chester Wenger echoed this sentiment in *Called to Be Sent*, a volume written in 1964 to celebrate the fiftieth anniversary of Eastern Mennonite Board of Missions: "Church cannot be separated from mission, for as the church goes about her business of witnessing she . . . becomes the church of Christ. . . . We cannot divide his church and his mission. . . . Only as we are in his mission as obedient disciples can we truly be in his church as faithful members of his body."[4] Churches that forget the mission inevitably perish.

Mennonite Member Profile 2006 asked members about the importance of service to those "within the church" and to those "outside the church," in an effort to gauge member commitments to either of these. Fifty percent said that service to others "within the church" is "very important" compared to 45% who said the same about serving those "outside the church."

Other questions inquired about the connections of congregations to their local communities and about member relationships to their congregations. When asked whether their "congregation touches the lives of many persons who live near it," both pastors and members were relatively pessimistic—29% of members completely agreeing with this statement and 27% of pastors. On several other missional indicators, members were more optimistic than their pastors. Thirty-eight percent of lay members completely agreed that their "congregation has a strong commitment to serve the local community," while only 25% of pastors believe the same. And where 37% of members completely agreed their "congregation has a clear sense of mission and purpose," only 23% of pastors said the same about their congregations.

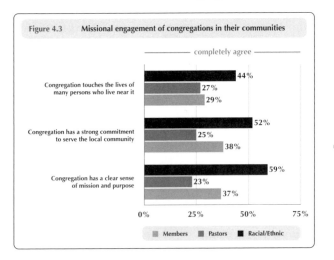

Figure 4.3   Missional engagement of congregations in their communities

Members also responded to questions about their relationship to their congregation and the quality of life within their congregation. Fifty-six percent of members and 61% of pastors completely agreed that "worship in my congregation helps me feel connected to a community of believers." Slightly over half of members (51%) completely agreed that they felt supported by their congregation (as did 60% of pastors). And fifty-four percent of members completely agreed that "my relationship with my congregation is very important to me" (69% of pastors).

Responses of members and pastors to these items show that they are more likely to agree that the congregation is meeting the needs of members than that it is connecting effectively to the local community. Racial/Ethnic members, however, are more connected to their local communities than Mennonites as a whole, perhaps because more Racial/Ethnic members live within the cities where their congregations are located. Forty-four percent of Racial/Ethnic members completely agree that their "congregation touches the lives of many persons who live near it" and 52% that their congregation "has a strong commitment to serve the local community." Fifty-nine percent believe that their "congregation has a clear sense of mission and purpose."

At the same time, however, Racial/Ethnic members, like Anglo members, are more likely to affirm the ministry of their congregations to members than to their local communities. Seventy-two percent of Racial/Ethnic members completely agree that their connections to their congregation were very important to them and 64% that they "feel personally supported" by their congregation. For all Mennonites, the struggle between being ministered to and ministering to others remains.

For men only. While pastors have often been seen as the ones with God's call and the responsibility to respond to that call, Mennonites—like many other denominations—historically believed that God's call was for men only. While Mennonite women actively served in leadership and ministry capacities in overseas or U.S. urban mission efforts, they were rarely affirmed or given opportunity to serve in the same roles at home. In fact, the sustainability of mission efforts frequently depended on the commitment of women to serve without recognition by the larger church and with substantial sacrifice. Many gave their lives to such service.

Today most area conferences of Mennonite Church USA ordain women. While only 17% of members in the denomination supported the ordination of women in 1972, support rose to 49% in 1989 and rests at 67% today. Among Mennonites ministers, 76% support the ordination of women and among Racial/Ethnic members, 71% support it. Regional differences reflect substantial diversity on this issue. Support is lowest in the East, where 52% of members favor the ordination of women, and highest in the

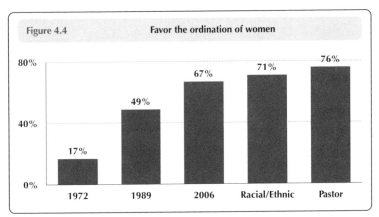

West (81%), followed by the Midwest (75%) and South (64%).

Although there is greater openness to the ordination of women today than in the past, members still prefer male leadership. Fifty-eight percent prefer a man as lead pastor of their congregation compared to 40% who have no preference and only 2% who prefer a woman. There is no significant difference between men and women in their gender preferences for pastoral leadership. While the ordination of women has freed women to use their gifts and callings in the church, the data suggest that it has not changed the deeper resistance of many members to having a woman minister in their own congregation—few members prefer a woman over a man.

If Mennonite congregations today are going to fulfill their callings to the world, it will necessitate a releasing of all the gifts of ministry regardless of gender, so that the words of the prophet Joel will come to life among us: "And afterward, I will pour out my Spirit on all people. Your sons and daughters will prophesy, your old men will dream dreams, your young men will see visions. Even on my servants, both men and women, I will pour out my Spirit in those days" (2:28-29).

No bag and no sandals. Part of the difficulty in obeying God's call to go is the lack of security and the high degree of uncertainty that so often comes with that call. Jeremiah certainly experienced his share of difficulty as he spoke God's words to those who could have cared less about Jeremiah or his God. There is much more security in being part of the church gathered on Sunday morning than in imagining ourselves as the church sent into the world throughout the week. Going where God calls will raise questions such as these: What we will say? Where will we go? How will we meet our needs? What will happen if no one receives us? Jesus did not give his disciples much satisfaction in response to such questions, sending them out in Luke 10 without any of the things that they probably thought were needed to do the work he was sending them to do.

In both 1989 and 2006, members were asked if they would be would be willing to move from their own community to help plant a new church. In 1989, 13% said they would be willing to move and another 25% agreed that they would be willing to help without moving. Fifty-five percent said they could only give money and 8% said they were not interested in planting new churches. In 2006, 10% said they would be willing to move, 20% to help without moving, and 48% to give money. Those not interested in church planting doubled to 22%. Racial/Ethnic members (55% of whom are U.S. immigrants), however, were almost three times more willing than members in the representative sample to move (29%) to help plant a church and less likely (34%) to only give money for such efforts. Undoubtedly the willingness of Racial/Ethnic members to move to plant a church is related to the fact that many of them are immigrants whose reality has been that of moving from place to place. Perhaps most Anglo Mennonites have been settled too long and have become too comfortable to hear the call. Interestingly, younger Mennonites, though relatively disengaged from the larger church, are also more willing to move to plant a church than are older Mennonites—18% compared to 8%.

Further analysis also shows a relationship between income and one's willingness to participate in a church plant. As one's household income increases, one is less willing to move in order to help plant a new church. Among Mennonites with annual household

Table 4.1	Interest in church planting among Mennonites			
Activity	1989	2006	Racial/Ethnic	Pastor
Willing to move	13	10	29	31
Will help but not move	25	20	22	33
Give money only	55	48	34	26
Not interested	8	22	16	10
		Percent		

incomes under $15,000, 20% would be willing to move, compared to only 5% of those who earned more than $200,000.

Afraid of strangers. Being called by God to a world in need creates anxiety simply because many of us are afraid of strangers. Mennonites in particular probably have good reason to be afraid of strangers, finding refuge in North America precisely because the strangers in Europe killed as many as forty thousand of our forebears. We have sufficient reason to believe that the world God might send us to is filled with dangerous people. But Americans in general are also becoming increasingly private and less civically engaged in their communities, spending little time on front porches and in their neighborhoods and more time in their homes, isolated in front of television and computer screens. As opportunities to nurture meaningful relationships decline, efforts to share Christ's love are also lost. Becoming a contrast community will require once again engaging the strangers around us.

In fact, data from Mennonite Member Profile 2006 shows that although Mennonites have become more like the broader society in lifestyle, few have close friends who are not Christians. When asked about their five closest friends outside their family, only 36% of members said that they had even one close friend who was not also part of a faith community, and fewer than one-fifth (18%) had *more than one* such friend. This means that most of us live our lives without meaningful connections to those who are not also members of a church. In this way, crossing boundaries to speak with strangers becomes a major obstacle to us, and one that only the most courageous are ever willing to confront.

Among new members of Mennonite congregations, however, one-half have at least one friend who is not a Christian, and 30% have two or more friends that are not. As we saw previously, new members are also more willing to evangelize non-Christians, probably in part because they know more of them than do other Mennonites.

Not for the wise and learned. Upon receiving the seventy-two disciples back from their mission in Luke 10, Jesus looked to heaven and thanked the Father for revealing the kingdom to children, not to the "wise and learned." While education is a gift that has often contributed to God's kingdom, educational achievements can also hinder obedience to the King. The problem for the wise and learned is that they are tempted to depend on their own wisdom and learning rather than to trust God's Spirit for guidance. The temptation is to follow Jesus in respectable, distinguished, and professional ways. But as Jeremiah learned when he responded to God's call, his reputation, respectability, and dignity were among the first things he lost.

Education does have some effect on personal evangelism and outreach efforts. Seventy-nine percent of college graduates agree that we should do all we can to convert nonbelievers, compared to 94% of those with no college degree. Among those with a college degree, 12% regularly make an effort to convert non-Christians while among non-college graduates 21% make such efforts. When it comes to inviting non-Christians to church activities, 9% of college graduates do so regularly, compared to 16% of those without a college degree. Those with a college degree are also less likely to support church-planting efforts than those without. While college graduates believe that the church should be engaged in evangelism, they personally are less committed to such efforts.

A Witness to Peace and Justice

A Mennonite witness to Jesus Christ has historically included a concern for social justice and peacemaking. This emphasis has been part of the historical "third way" of Anabaptists that has distinguished us from most other Christian traditions. To what extent do Mennonites today care about issues of peacemaking and social justice as part of their witness for Christ?

When Mennonite respondents were asked, "Is there any important way in which Mennonites seem different to you from other Christians?" 37% replied no, a similar percentage found for those who do not identify themselves as either Mennonite or Anabaptist. The nearly two-thirds who do see Mennonites as distinctive were then asked to describe the differences they saw. In other words, what did they perceive to be the core values of Mennonites today?

Their open-ended responses most often mentioned "nonviolence and peace," with 30% saying something along this line. Mentioned next, but much less frequently were the following:
- a close community of people (7%)
- service to others (7%)
- simple lifestyles (6%)
- social justice (5%)

In addition, Mennonites seem to connect their views on peacemaking to Jesus. When asked about the "most important reason for peacemaking," 73% said cited "Jesus' life and teaching as a peacemaker" compared to only 10% who pointed to "the practical reality that violence is not effective."

Members strongly support Christian witness in forms such as Mennonite Central Committee's efforts to engage the U.S. government and the United Nations on war, peace, poverty, and social justice. Eighty-two percent of members support this type of witness and 85% believe that "church leaders should try to influence government leaders on issues like war, peace, racism, and poverty."

When given a list of fourteen items that reflect possible faith commitments, 50% of members said that "peacemaking and nonviolence" are very important while 34% said that "evangelizing non-believers" is very important. These two—peacemaking and evangelization—were consistently held together by members (including Racial/Ethnic members) and pastors when asked about the priorities of the denomination and its agencies.

In choosing the three most important activities that Mennonite Church USA should be engaged in from a list of six, members most frequently selected "sharing God's love in word and deed" (81%), and working for peace and justice (53%). Racial/Ethnic members also ranked these two most highly.

Table 4.2	The most important activities of Mennonite Church USA		
Activity	**2006**	**Racial/Ethnic**	**Pastor**
Peace and justice	53	50	33
Missional church	36	31	53
Equipping members	38	36	62
Partnering globally	31	28	30
God's love in word and deed	81	76	81
Developing leaders	37	41	43
		Percent	

When asked about the "most important thing Mennonite mission agencies should be doing in the United States and abroad," 73% of members marked "doing both evangelism and social ministry," compared to 11% who marked just evangelism and 16% who indicated the meeting of economic and social needs. The response was similar from Racial/Ethnic members.

Finally, when given a list of eight priorities for Mennonite mission agencies and asked to list the three highest, two were clearly most important to respondents: "global evangelism and church planting" (55%), followed by "peacemaking and reconciliation" (48%). These were the two highest priorities for Racial/Ethnic members and pastors as well.

Despite assimilation into the broader culture and greater politicization in the church, these findings confirm that Mennonites in the United States have retained some residue of their historic com-

Table 4.3	Priorities for Mennonite mission agencies		
Activity	2006	Racial/ Ethnic	Pastor
Evangelizing	11	20	10
Economic/social needs	16	12	4
Evangelism and social/ economic needs	73	67	86
Do not support mission work	0	1	0
		Percent	

mitments to peace and justice and that they consistently hold these commitments alongside a concern for evangelistic activity. Mennonites strongly affirm that their witness to Christ should be holistic—concerned with the salvation of individuals and the transformation of society.

Conclusion

The findings in this chapter reveal several things about Mennonites today. First, members continue to embrace the unique witness to peace and social justice. Their commitment is also, at least at some level, connected to their understanding of Jesus. Concern for peacemaking does not seem to have eroded commitments to evangelism, outreach, and church planting as church-wide priorities. In fact, nearly three-quarters (73%) agree that both should be a priority, with only 18% believing that peacemaking and reconciliation should be a priority but not evangelism.

Second, while members strongly affirm church planting and evangelism as important denominational priorities, few are making much effort to be evangelistic in their own lives with neighbors, friends, or co-workers—with the exception of Racial/Ethnic members. In fact, few Mennonites have close friends who are not Christians, adding to the challenge of communicating the gospel effectively.

Third, Mennonite congregations do not appear to be primarily focused on their surrounding communities, and they tend to rate their internal congregational activity more highly than the work they are doing outside the congregation.

Fourth, members tend to see their pastors as the primary "ministers" and resist becoming ministers themselves. Church remains largely a place to be ministered to rather than to be prepared for ministry for the coming week. And while a majority of members support the ordination of women, few prefer a female pastor, thus continuing to limit the expression of women's gifts in the church.

Fifth, outside of Racial/Ethnic members, few Mennonites appear willing to make much sacrifice to become involved in church planting efforts. While many are willing to donate money, most are unwilling to move to another community to plant a church. And fewer are interested in church planting today than in 1989.

As I visited Racial/Ethnic pastors and congregations during this study, it became clear that these members and congregations are strongly committed to reaching their communities with the good news of the gospel. Hispanic congregations in Chicago, for example, prominently display murals in their sanctuaries of the Chicago skyline and proclaim their call to proclaim Christ. Their vision statements are displayed for all to see. In one Indonesian congregation of 150 members in Philadelphia, founded in 2005, visitors are immediately greeted with a headset that translates the service into English. Though the congregation is almost completely Indonesian today, its leaders articulate a strong vision for reaching their multiethnic community for Christ and for becoming a multicultural congregation. The pastor put their vision this way: "Our desire is to reach more than Indonesians, especially our neighborhood where there are many African-Americans, whites, and many Asians who don't go to church and even sometimes don't know about God and Jesus. That scares me. And that's the challenge for us as a church. What is the church building? What is the church if we can not reach them? It's useless!"

One has little doubt about the vision and mission of these congregations and pastors to do what they describe as "kingdom" work. And the growth they are experiencing is testimony to God's blessing on their efforts.

I also found that urban Racial/Ethnic congregations, more than other Mennonite congregations, effectively combine evangelistic outreach with social action. They do not appear to be torn between these two callings, but live in contexts where they are daily faced with the realities that Jesus Christ is the answer both for broken individuals and for unjust social and political structures. The immediacy of need in urban areas demands an approach that addresses the transformation of individuals and of social structures and relationships. As one African-American pastor explained:

> We affirm and understand that reconciliation and shalom are of value right here and right now. In our urban setting of Philadelphia with three-hundred-plus murders last year, that message is actually a message that is welcome, if indeed we are able to get outside of our church walls and communicate that. But what do we do about it? Do we just read the news and sit on the sidelines and run from our cars into our churches and pray and then run back to our cars and go home? There are some days I feel like doing that, but the reality is we cannot. If we are going to be followers of Jesus Christ, we can't just sit by idly on the side lines. So for us, it's looking at concrete ways that we as a congregation can impact violence in the city of Philadelphia.

The power of Jeremiah's message lay in the imagination that God gave him to see a reality beyond the disruption of Judah and Jerusalem that was coming. By letting go of the past, Jeremiah could see and speak about a new future that God was preparing. The question for Mennonites today is, Can we imagine new missional possibilities for ourselves, our congregations, and our denomination? Can we imagine the following?

- A future where all of our congregations have standing room only?
- A future where our children and grandchildren want to be engaged in "kingdom" work more than anything else in the world?
- A future where healing and reconciliation in families, communities, and across racial and ethnic lines are commonplace?

- A future where the poor, the aliens, and those on the margins are cared for and find hope?
- A future where congregational offerings are so large that church agencies have annual surpluses to invest in new ministries?
- A future where we have no choice but to plant new churches because the ones we have are overflowing?
- A future where God's presence is as fully expressed when we are gathered together as when we are sent into the world?
- A future that connects us with other believers in our community, Mennonite or not, who are being obedient to the call of being sent to the world?
- A future where all races and ethnicities worship and serve together—exhibiting the shalom of God's kingdom?

Or are our imaginations stuck where we are? Are we limited by our fears of what appears to be reality? Or even worse, are we content with where we are and with the current status of the church? If congregations are going to become fully engaged in God's mission, their members will need to take the lead, stepping outside of the comfort of their daily routines and embracing God's call to go wherever God sends.

Jesus' final words before his ascension were sending words, echoing those of his sending in Luke 10. And I suspect his first questions when we enter heaven will be related to our obedience to that call: "Child, were you sent? Did you proclaim peace to their homes? Did you announce that the kingdom of God was near? Did you trample on snakes and scorpions? Did you overcome all the power of the enemy? Did Satan fall?"

5

God's Words—Then and Now

In the eighth year of this reign, while [Josiah] was still young, he began to seek the God of his father David. . . . In the eighteenth year of Josiah's reign . . . he sent Shaphan son of Azaliah and Maaseiah the ruler of the city, with Joah . . . the recorder, to repair the temple of the LORD his God. . . .

While they were bringing out the money that had been taken into the temple of the LORD, Hilkiah the priest found the Book of the Law of the Lord. . . . Then Shaphan took the book to the king. . . . When the king heard the words of the Law, he tore his robes. He gave these orders. . . . "Go and inquire of the LORD for me and for the remnant in Israel and Judah about what is written in this book that has been found. Great is the LORD's anger that is poured out on us because our fathers have not kept the word of the LORD." —2 Chronicles 34:3, 8, 14, 16, 19-21

In the fourth year of Jehoiakim son of Josiah king of Judah, this word came to Jeremiah from the LORD: "Take a scroll and write on it all the words I have spoken to you concerning Israel, Judah and all other nations from the time I began speaking to you in the reign of Josiah till now. Perhaps when the people of Judah hear about every disaster I plan to inflict on them, each of them will turn from his wicked way; then I will forgive their wickedness and their sin. . . .

After they put the scroll in the room of Elishama the secretary, they went to the king in the courtyard and reported everything to him. The king sent Jehudi to get the scroll, and Jehudi brought it from the room of Elishama and read it to the king and all the officials. . . . It was the ninth month and the king was sitting in the winter apartment, with a fire burning in the firepot in front of him. Whenever Jehudi had read three or four columns of the scroll, the king cut them off with a scribe's knife and threw them into the firepot, until the entire scroll was burned in the fire.
—Jeremiah 36:1-3, 20-23

No two responses to God's words could be more different than these of father and son—Josiah and Jehoiakim. In the first story, Hilkiah the priest has just discovered the Book of the Law while renovating the temple. Listening to Shaphan the secretary read God's words from this long-lost scroll, Josiah responds with terror at the unfaithfulness of God's people and the judgment it will surely bring. In the second passage, Josiah's son Jehoiakim reacts just as passionately as his father to God's words through Jeremiah. But his response is passionate rejection. For the words of God, whenever and wherever they are spoken, usually turn us one way or another—away from God or away from ourselves. But regardless of our response, God's words endure, and so Jeremiah and Baruch faithfully rewrote the scroll following Jehoiakim's outburst, adding even more of God's words to a second draft.

In an era where biblical criticism has deadened the living words of God, Walter Brueggemann challenges our tendency to read the Scripture as simply one more text among millions of others. Too many of us read the Bible with the same eyes and ears by which we read all other information today—newspapers, fairy tales, Internet hoaxes, or encyclopedias—and too often perhaps with the same expectations. The biblical narrative alone holds the source of life, and opening ourselves to God's Spirit in those words provides the key.[1]

Words of Life

The danger as postmodern human beings is our tendency to disconnect the biblical narrative from our lives and experience and in the process to be uninspired and unimaginative in our interpretation and application of the Scriptures. Too often we treat the Bible as an object to disagree or agree with, as a science book to be held up to empirical evidence, as a list of commands to be checked off as done or not done, or as ammunition for our ongoing theological debates.

Periodically we hear Sunday school teachers or others suggest that, rather than the Bible, we should teach our children about the real issues of life—something contemporary and up-to-date. After all, many of our children already know the stories, perhaps even by memory. While most of us might not say this so directly, I think many of us live with a similar view of God's words. We affirm that intellectual awareness of the Bible is important, but we have long ago given up confidence that its contents can address the complex problems of the twenty-first century. We fail to recognize that the Bible was written not primarily as a source of information to be read, memorized, and put on a mental shelf somewhere but as a spring of living water that still gives daily life and direction. In this way, many of us function more as atheists than true believers, missing out on the power and authority that we say are ours in Christ and in the Scripture.

Failing to imagine our own lives and experiences within the stories of the Bible denies the power of the Spirit—who first spoke these words—to bring them alive in the hearts of old and young, rich and poor, liberal and conservative. Placing our lives in the biblical narrative continually reminds us of God's plans and purposes for our lives and our congregations. Doing so, our lives take on transcendent value and purpose that is often forgotten in the context of our day-to-day struggles. Interjecting ourselves into the biblical stories raises the stakes dramatically but also heightens the meaning of our existence.

Words to Dwell In

In *Texts that Linger, Words that Explode*, Brueggemann relates what can happen from time to time to those children in Sunday school class yawning with boredom and twitching restlessly in their seat. If we keep telling those stories and challenging listeners to pay attention to them, the stories will from time to time

> erupt into new usage . . . the words of the text seize someone in the community. . . . In that moment of re-utterance, the present is freshly illuminated, reality is irreversibly transformed. The community comes to know or see or receive or decide afresh. What has been tradition, hovering in dormancy, becomes available experience. In the moment of speaking and hearing, this is treasured tradition now become present experience.[2]

This is the kind of transformation and awakening that living within God's words can bring. But as our data shows many of us have little time to engage the Scripture at all, let alone at a level that ignites our bodies and our souls. And without taking the time to do so, in daily devotions, personal retreat, or small group study, the words of God remain dead letters in our lives and experiences.

A key practice of congregations that have committed to becoming missional is that of "Dwelling in the Word," in which every meeting or gathering begins by reading a passage of Scripture, with participants gathering in pairs to discuss what was heard, and then sharing what was heard with others.[3] This practice has transformed congregations and staff who have engaged in it. A key passage for missional churches is Luke 10, where Jesus sends the seventy-two disciples in pairs to announce the kingdom of God and to carry the kingdom's peace (shalom). Dwelling in this and other passages begins to shape individuals and congregations. As they live within God's Word, they find that the Scripture begins to "read" them rather than they the Scripture. That is, through the words of God the Spirit of God begins to speak into their lives, showing them what God is calling them to do and who God is calling them to be—convicting, challenging, teaching, and sending them into the world with the gospel.[4]

Words for Resistance

Brueggemann also reminds us that the words of God have power to confront the principalities and powers of evil and the devil. Jeremiah faithfully used the power of the scroll in challenging the kings of Judah and Israel with their unrighteousness and injustice. The use of "scroll power" was Jesus' only defense against the "seduction of the devil" in the desert, where he repeatedly invoked God's words.[5] The scroll of God, arguably more than any other in all of history, has time and again ignited social and spiritual reform (as in Josiah's reign) and resistance against the powers of injustice and evil. Major social movements, including the Protestant Reformation, the Civil Rights Movement in the United States, and various foreign political revolutions of the late twentieth century relied upon "scroll power." In these places and times, Brueggemann notes, "the Bible has been an impetus, a summons, an authorization to undertake bold action, which may be revolutionary or subversive . . . the text keeps surfacing as a 'weapon of the weak.'"[6]

The power of God's words (the scroll) to empower resistance against injustice is one reason Philip Jenkins, author of *The New Faces of Christianity: Believing the Bible in the Global South*, argues that the Bible has more meaning for those who live in the global south than for those north of the equator (Europe and North America particularly).[7] For Christians in Africa, Asia, and Latin America, the cultural and historical realities (such as poverty, persecution, and powerlessness) out of which the Scriptures were written make the Bible easier to identify with than for North Americans or Europeans whose reality has been shaped by the Enlightenment, affluence, and privilege.

The reality of life for southern hemisphere Christians, says Jenkins, keeps the Scripture alive and empowers them to confront poverty and injustice. North Americans and Europeans (particularly those who are white), on the other hand, read the Scripture through postmodern lenses that too often do not take seriously the radical and costly claims of Scripture. Nor are most North Americans and Europeans interested in resisting or confronting political and social structures that have given and protected their power, status, and affluence.

Mennonites Today

Mennonites have historically been known as people who take seriously the words of God, and in particular, those of the Word made flesh and made known to us in the New Testament. But how true is this of Mennonites in the United States today? To what extent do God's words direct our lives? In what way is our theology— proclaimed and lived—grounded in our understanding of Scripture? Do we react to God's words with repentance or with resistance? How do we spiritually discern God's words? What do we believe about Scripture? How have our views about God's words changed over time?

In this chapter we are going to consider, based upon findings from Mennonite Member Profile 2006, how Mennonites hear God —through Scripture, through prayer, through their experiences, and through spiritual discernment in the community of faith.

Beliefs About God

Beliefs about how God speaks are likely related to what one believes about God in the first place. Belief in God is high among Mennonites and has remained so across three decades. The vast majority (87%) of members today believe that "God really exists" and "have no doubts about it," compared to 89% who said the same in 1972. While 12% today acknowledge doubts about God, this is only 3% more than in 1972. Belief in God among Mennonites mirrors that of conservative Protestants, 83% of whom express belief without doubts, and is higher than among mainline Protestants (60%).[8]

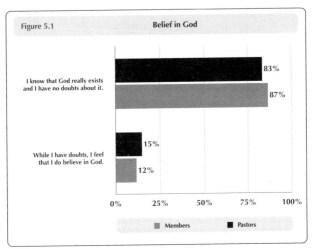

Figure 5.1   Belief in God

I know that God really exists and I have no doubts about it. 83% 87%

While I have doubts, I feel that I do believe in God. 15% 12%

0%   25%   50%   75%   100%

■ Members   ■ Pastors

Sixty-seven percent of members describe their relationship as close or very close to God compared to 54% in 1972. More than half (51%) of Mennonites believe that God "controls most of the events in my daily life" and another 44% that God "guides me, but does not control the events of my daily life." Members feel much more positively about masculine images of God than feminine ones. Nearly three-fourths (73%) of Mennonites feel negatively about references to God as "Mother" or "she" and only 10% feel positively. On the other hand, 76% feel positively about references to God as "Father" or "he" and only 5% feel negatively.

Jesus. Members were asked a wide variety of questions about Jesus. Sixty-nine percent of Mennonites, when asked about the uniqueness of Jesus, believe that "Jesus is the only way to God and that those without faith in Jesus will not be saved." Another 24% believe that "Jesus is the clearest revelation of God but that God may save persons who do not know Jesus." Fewer than 7% believe that "Jesus is one of many ways to God" or that Jesus was nothing more than "a great teacher or prophet."

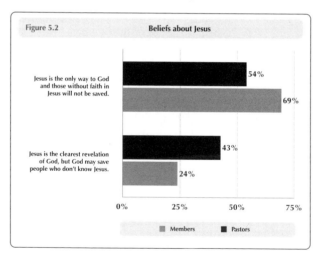

Figure 5.2   Beliefs about Jesus

When given a choice of four reasons for Jesus' death and asked to choose the one that most reflects their view, members showed little evidence of having been influenced by "atonement" debates among Mennonite scholars, with 85% saying that "Jesus had to die to complete God's plan of salvation." Other categories and responses were as follows:

- Jesus died as a sacrifice to satisfy God's anger against sin: 4%
- Jesus willingly died to show the power of nonviolent love: 9%
- Jesus died because he condemned social and economic injustice: 2%

Pastors, however, were less likely to say that "Jesus had to die to complete God's plan of salvation," with only 64% agreeing with this statement and 24% choosing that "Jesus willingly died to show the power of nonviolent love" (compared to 9% of members).

Nearly two-thirds (64%) of Mennonites say that they have a close personal relationship with Christ and that this relationship is the "centerpiece" of their faith story. Only 3% said that a close personal relationship with Christ has no part in their faith story, and the remaining 33% that it is "one part of my faith story."

Ninety-eight percent of Mennonites have accepted Jesus Christ as Savior and Lord. For 49% of them, this acceptance occurred during a "specific moment" in time. For another 49% of members, this acceptance was "gradual." Mennonite pastors, however, were more likely to report a specific moment of conversation (59%). Seventy-eight percent of Mennonites describe themselves as born again, though there is regional variation. Mennonites in the East (89%) are most likely to be born again and those in the Midwest (71%) and West (72%) least likely. When conservative Protestants in the United States were asked a similar question, 65% said they were born again, compared to 36% of mainline Protestants.[9]

Respondents were provided with a list of six "views of Jesus" and asked to check all that applied to them. They answered as follows:

	Percent with this view
• I think of Jesus as my personal Lord and Savior.	81%
• I seek to be a disciple of Jesus in my daily living.	74%
• I eagerly anticipate Jesus' return to earth.	43%
• I think of Jesus as a nonviolent peacemaker.	43%
• I think of Jesus as a radical social activist.	15%
• I think of Jesus in a fairly general way.	4%

These responses show that Mennonite members tend to think of Jesus most as their Lord and Savior, and very closely behind, as one whom they follow in everyday life. Fewer members think much about Jesus' return or think of Jesus as peacemaker or a radical social activist.

Responses from members varied depending on how they defined their religious identity, with those who identify as Mennonite or Anabaptist less likely than evangelicals or fundamentalists to eagerly anticipate Jesus' return, and to view Jesus as their personal Lord and Savior. Not surprisingly, Anabaptists/Mennonites were more likely to view Jesus as a nonviolent peacemaker and as a radical social activist than evangelical/fundamentalists.

Table 5.1	Beliefs about Jesus by religious identity	
	Anabaptist/ Mennonite	Evangelical/ Fundamentalist
I seek to be a daily disciple	78	83
I anticipate Jesus' return	41	56
Jesus is my Lord and Savior	80	89
Jesus is a nonviolent peacemaker	49	37
Jesus is a radical social activist	18	11
	Percent	

Nine out of ten Mennonites affirm that "Jesus was born of a virgin" (92%) and that "Jesus physically rose from the dead" (94%), but a fewer number that "Jesus will physically return to earth some day" (83%).

These beliefs about Jesus have changed relatively little since the first member profile, when 94% of members affirmed the virgin birth of Jesus and 90% his physical resurrection. Mennonites are only slightly less certain today that there is a place of eternal punishment (83% believed in 1972 compared to 78% in 2006) but more uncertain that the "devil is active in the world today" (95% agreed in 1972 compared to 82% today).

The Holy Spirit. Mennonites overwhelmingly (97%) affirm that the "Holy Spirit is active in the world today." But what members believe about how the Spirit works and moves are quite different. When given four choices to describe the Holy Spirit's work, 68% of members selected the "Holy Spirit speaks to individuals directly and also through the faith community." One-fourth believe that the "Spirit speaks directly to individuals in a personal way."

The response of Racial/Ethnic members to this question was more evenly split between these two responses, with 45% choosing "the Spirit speaks directly to individuals in a personal way" while 51% that "the Spirit speaks to individuals directly and also through the faith community."

Experience of the charismatic gifts. While nearly all Mennonites affirm the work of the Holy Spirit in the world and that the Holy Spirit still speaks to people today, they are divided in their understanding of how the Spirit manifests its presence. When asked their "view of the charismatic gifts of the Holy Spirit, such as healing, prophesying and speaking in tongues," 61% said they "are genuine gifts of God's Spirit to some Christians." Mennonites in the East (70%) and South (68%) are most likely to believe this and those in the Midwest least likely at 53%. Among Racial/Ethnic members, 83% chose this response, again showing the differences between Racial/Ethnic members and other Mennonites in their experience of the Spirit.

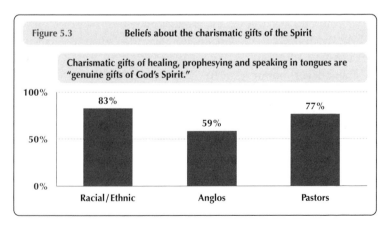

Figure 5.3   Beliefs about the charismatic gifts of the Spirit

Charismatic gifts of healing, prophesying and speaking in tongues are "genuine gifts of God's Spirit."

Members were asked whether they had "ever personally experienced any of these gifts of the Spirit"—casting out demons, speaking in tongues, prophesying, receiving the baptism of the Holy Spirit, and healing someone. Forty-four percent of Mennonites as a whole have experienced these gifts at one time or another in their lives, compared to 70% of Racial/Ethnic members.

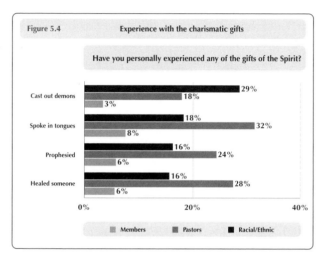

Figure 5.4   Experience with the charismatic gifts

Have you personally experienced any of the gifts of the Spirit?

	Members	Pastors	Racial/Ethnic
Cast out demons	3%	18%	29%
Spoke in tongues	8%	18%	32%
Prophesied	6%	16%	24%
Healed someone	6%	16%	28%

Of members who have experienced these gifts of the Spirit, 33% have received the baptism of the Holy Spirit, 8% have spoken in tongues, 6% have prophesied, 6% have healed someone, and 3% have cast out demons. But only 23% of these persons have experienced these gifts within the past year, while for 62% of members the experience was more than five years ago.

Among Racial/Ethnic members who have experienced the charismatic gifts, these experiences were more recent—47% within the last year and 16% within the past five years. Receiving the Spirit was experienced most (53%) followed by casting out demons (29%), speaking in tongues (18%), prophesy (16%), and healing (16%).

Pastors are more like Racial/Ethnic members in their experiences of the Holy Spirit than are other members. Seventy-seven percent of pastors believe that the charismatic gifts of the Holy

Spirit are "genuine gifts of God's Spirit to some Christians" compared to 61% of members. And 66% of pastors (compared to
44% of members) have personally experienced charismatic gifts,
including casting out demons, speaking in tongues, prophesying,
the baptism of the Holy Spirit, and healing. Forty-six percent of
pastors state that these experiences have been within the past year.

The percentage of members who have experienced the charismatic gifts has remained about the same since 1972, when 5%
reported speaking in tongues compared to 7% in 1989 and 8% in
2006. Experiences of prophesy and casting out demons were up
slightly also.

Scripture. Almost four-fifths (79%) of Mennonites believe that
"the miracles in the Bible are historical facts" and 62% that "God
performs the same kind of miracles today as in the Bible." Fifty-
seven percent believe that the "Bible is the inspired Word of God,
but that not everything in it should be taken literally," while another 36% believe that the "Bible is the actual Word of God and is to
be taken literally, word for word." Only 6% of Mennonites believe
the Bible is "an ancient book of stories, history, and moral guidelines," and none believe that the "Bible has no relevance for
today." Regionally, 45% of eastern Mennonites believe in a literal,
word-for-word Bible compared to 37% of southern and western
Mennonites and 31% of Midwestern Mennonites. Racial/Ethnic
members were more likely than other members to believe that the
Bible is to be taken literally, word for word (65%).

Mennonite beliefs about the Bible have changed over three
decades. While the question wording differed slightly in the 1972
and 2006 member surveys, the trend shows movement away from
an understanding of the Scripture as "infallible" to one that affirms
the Scripture as God's inspired word not to be taken literally word
for word.

Among other Americans, 54% of conservative Protestants say
that the Bible is the actual word of God to be taken literally word
for word compared to 26% of mainline Protestants. A literal
interpretation of Scripture has also declined among conservative

Protestants over the past two decades, from 62% in 1984 to 47% in 2002.[10]

In an effort to tap whether Mennonites have a "flat" view of the Scripture or one that sees all of Scripture through Christ, members were asked which Testament in the Bible has the highest authority— Old or New? Fifty-three percent reported the New Testament and 45% said that both have equal authority. Only 1% indicated that the Old Testament has the highest authority. When asked which part of the New Testament influenced them the most, 45% marked all parts equally, 40% marked the Gospels, 10% the letters of Paul, and 5% other books in the New Testament. Pastors (73%) were more likely than members to say that the New Testament has the greatest authority and that the Gospels have influenced them the most of all New Testament books (60%).

Spiritual Practices

Hearing God's voice requires spiritual practices that nurture a listening for that voice. Members were asked a number of questions about their practice of various spiritual disciplines.

Prayer. Three-quarters of Mennonites pray daily. This compares nationally with 71% of conservative Protestants who report praying daily and 54% of mainline Protestants.[11] Unlike Bible reading, there appear to be relatively few differences in who prays and how much.

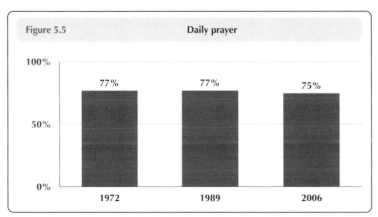

Figure 5.5   Daily prayer

Prayer has remained the same for Mennonites across three decades, with 77% of members in 1972 reporting that they prayed daily, compared to 75% today.

Bible Reading. While Mennonites generally have a high view of Scripture, relatively few read the Bible on a daily basis (32%). Sixty-nine percent read the Bible at least weekly. The proportion of Mennonites who read the Bible daily has remained constant over the last two decades.

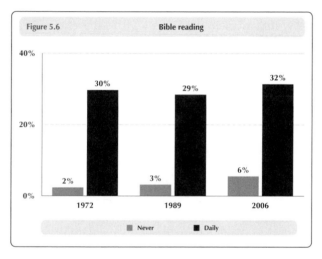

Figure 5.6   Bible reading

Mennonite rates of reading the Bible, however, are higher than among other American Christians. Twenty-one percent of conservative Protestants read the Bible daily, as do 14% of mainline Protestants.[12]

Spiritual Discernment

Mennonite Member Profile 2006 asked several questions that measure the extent to which respondents were open to spiritually discerning the Holy Spirit's direction with other believers. That is, do Mennonites value the faith community in decision making, or are they as individualistic as other Americans in their attitudes about faith and religion? Do they value and practice listening for direction by the Holy Spirit within the context of the community of faith? While 79% reported that they "seek the Holy Spirit's guidance" at least once a week, does any of this seeking occur within the community of faith?

Church involvement. While the percentage of Mennonites who regularly attend church has remained about the same since 1972, church attendance for Mennonites has become largely a "once a week" event, with the percentage who attend more than once a week dropping from 43% in 1972 to 8% today. In addition, the proportion who attend Sunday school has declined from 71% in 1972 to 53% today.

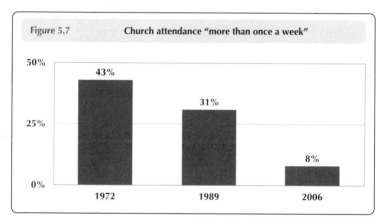

Figure 5.7   Church attendance "more than once a week"

Church attendance for Mennonites varies by region of the country, with 86% of Mennonites in the East attending every Sunday, compared to 77% in both the Midwest and West. Sunday school attendance is lowest in the West (42% every week) and highest in the East (61%) and South (62%).

Just over one-third (38%) of Mennonites participate in a small group that meets at least two or three times a month for "discussion, prayer, or Bible study," compared to 71% of Racial/Ethnic members. The percent of members who regularly participated in small groups in 1989 was 43%. In general, Mennonites are spending less time in church than in previous years.

Church accountability. When provided with a list of fourteen statements and asked how important each was to their faith commitment, 28% said that "giving and receiving counsel from other members" was "very important." Of all fourteen statements, this one was least important to respondents, except for "living a simple lifestyle," which only 27% agree is "very important." The list of statements and member responses were:

Figure 5.8	Importance of statements to member's faith commitment

	Percent
Following Jesus in daily life	83
Expressing Christian love in all my relationships	71
Praising and glorifying God	70
Adult baptism	57
Practicing the spiritual disciplines	54
Peacemaking and nonviolence	50
Serving others within the church	50
Serving others outside the church	45
Building strong bonds of community in the church	44
Evangelizing nonbelievers	34
Nonconformity to the world	30
Promoting social justice in the world	29
Giving and receiving counsel from other members	28
Living a simple lifestyle	27

Members were asked the extent to which they agreed with several statements related to the church, again in an effort to measure an openness to the discernment of others versus a more individualistic spirituality. The percentage who agreed with the following statements are listed below:
- The organized church does not really matter; personal faith is what counts: 38%.
- Mennonite congregations should have clear guidelines for membership: 83%.
- The church has no business being involved in my personal lifestyle decisions: 19%.
- Faith is a private matter between me and God: 56%.

These responses suggest some ambivalence about the church's involvement in member lives. On the one hand, members want the church to have clear guidelines, even while believing that faith is a private matter. Member responses to these questions also suggest that while members believe that their congregation has the right to interfere with lifestyle decisions, members value a private faith. These polarities—individual faith and community accountability—create tension in processes of spiritual discernment within congregations. Perhaps members are reflecting the desire that their congregations have guidelines for other members, but not for themselves!

Competition from Other Voices

Peter Berger, a well-known sociologist of religion, has argued that a traditional society can maintain itself over time only if a society manages to communicate its words in "one voice." In other words, any society that hopes to sustain itself must communicate its values and beliefs in a unified way that is reinforced by multiple institutions, such as the family, religion, and education.[13]

The success of the Old Order Amish at sustaining their culture for more than three hundred years is rooted in their ability to speak as one voice and to minimize voices from outside their culture. Following the tragic school shootings of five Amish girls in October 2006, Amish individuals echoed in unison their forgiveness of the man who had killed their daughters. Few, if any, Amish voices challenged this larger voice. Listening to church leaders, parents, grandparents, teachers, friends, and neighbors all saying the same thing generation after generation about forgiveness prepared Amish individuals for this tragic event and gives them power to resist temptations of the "world" around them. While other Christians sometimes criticize the Amish for their lack of evangelical witness, no community has ever spoken so loudly and to so many as the Amish about Christian forgiveness in the face of violence. The corporate witness of the Amish may echo long after many other individual voices have passed.

Postmodern individuals, however, find ourselves confronted constantly by societal voices that do not agree with one another and that often challenge the truth of God's voice. The nation competes for our allegiance to God. Advertisers compete for our loyalty and money. The media compete for our listening and watching. Even within our communities of faith, various religious voices compete for our attention—evangelical, charismatic, liberal, conservative, Anabaptist, fundamentalist, and more. More than any generation before us, we are subject to and engage freely in a multitude of diverse voices. Inundated by words and information, we are a people who seem beyond the point of listening as one community of faith or of articulating in one voice—a major reason for our struggle with questions of Mennonite and Anabaptist identity.

More assimilated into the broader culture and society than ever before, Mennonites are listening to a wider number of voices even while spending less time at church. When we asked members about the voices that they hear at least several times a week, we learned this:

- 47% listen to Christian radio
- 36% listen to National Public Radio
- 15% watch religious programs on television
- 15% listen to Focus on the Family
- 27% watch sports on TV
- 72% watch news on TV
- 6% watch MTV or Comedy Central
- 77% read newspapers or magazines
- 59% read or study their Bible
- 53% read books
- 10% watch movies (at home or in a theater)
- 31% regularly read *The Mennonite* and
- 26% the *Mennonite Weekly Review*

Ninety-seven percent of Mennonites have a television in their home and 73% have an Internet connection. In a typical day, Mennonites who watch television do so for 2.4 hours and those who use the Internet at home do so for 1.3 hours. In 1972, 18% of Mennonites watched no television in a typical week compared to 9% today. Forty-eight percent watched one hour or less per day in 1972 compared to 18% in 2006 who watch as little. And of course, no one had the Internet in 1972.

When asked about their activities on the Internet, 65% read

e-mail, 34% buy things, 31% read the news, 26% do banking, 25% receive church information, and 14% look for religious information. Only 2% do online blogging, and 11% send instant messages. Over the past year, 9% of members report viewing an X-rated movie and 7% visited a pornographic Web site. These findings for Mennonites seem to confirm what others have said about American Christians— that they spend much more time watching television than in prayer, Bible reading, and worship.[14]

Conclusion

God's people have always struggled with the temptation to obey voices other than that of their Creator. But God continually gives opportunities to respond to his words. When the scroll was found in the temple, Josiah reacted with repentance and a recommitment to God. Having given in to the voices of strangers and foreigners, worshipping other gods and living for pleasure, wealth, and privilege, everything changed on the day that the scroll was found as Josiah tore his clothes in grief and agony at God's words. And because of Josiah's tender heart and humility, the prophetess Huldah stated that God would withhold judgment against Judah during Josiah's lifetime. Within just one generation, however, Josiah's recommitment to God's words was lost, as his own son Jehoiakim violently rejected God's words through Jeremiah the prophet.

In the midst of many competing voices, this chapter suggests a number of conclusions about Mennonites today.

Mennonites remain firmly committed to a belief in God. The orthodoxy of their beliefs in Jesus—the virgin birth and a physical resurrection—have changed little over time. Clearly, Mennonites are not "unbelievers." This belief, however, lacks an equivalent commitment to spiritual practices that nurture the hearing of God's voice. While Mennonites, like most Americans, report praying daily, less than one-third read the Scriptures as frequently. Mennonites attend church less than ever before, with most going only on Sunday morning. And just over one-third participate in a regular small group. At the same time, Mennonite members are more in tune with voices outside their churches and homes than Mennonites in the past, spending more than two hours daily watching television and one hour on the Internet at home. The multitude of voices competing with that of God and the church is clear.

Mennonite members are ambivalent about the role of the church in providing accountability for their religious beliefs and commitments. Members believe that the church should provide guidelines for living, but do not value the giving and receiving of counsel to which most are asked to submit as part of their baptismal vows. Like other Americans, faith for many Mennonites is an increasingly private and personal matter.

The gap between active prayer and active Scripture reading is cause for reflection. How can we pray effectively and hear God's Spirit in our prayers when we are disconnected from the words of God? This chasm between frequently speaking our own words to God but rarely listening to God's words is a manifestation of postmodern American spirituality, a spirituality that is often undisciplined and individualistic—on my own terms and in my own time. Separating our hearts and minds from the words of God silences the scroll power that overcomes evil of all kinds (demons, injustice, abuse, and all expressions of the principalities and powers). Prayer without the words of God leaves us weakened, crippled, and alienated, rather than individuals engaged in a community of faith that crosses time and space. The need to hear God's words is more important than ever before. Mennonites are becoming increasingly assimilated, with higher levels of education and more professional occupations, while at the same time becoming less involved in their local congregations.

So, who will find the scroll today? Who will reclaim the words of God today? Where is Josiah? Where are the prophets and prophetesses, like Jeremiah and Huldah, who will speak the meaning of God's words? To what extent do we have any chance of hearing God or one another given the din of so many other voices and words in our world? Is there any chance that Mennonites—parents, grandparents, pastors, Sunday school teachers, counselors—can reclaim the voice of God? Can we resist the influences that are shaping us? Can we at least minimize them in some way?

These and many other questions remain to be answered. Those who are open to the disruptive work of God's Spirit and who can commit to being sent into the world on behalf of the kingdom are those most likely to find the answers. Their lives will become the answers as they alone incarnate the living words of God.

6

Homeland Security

"Woe to him who builds his palace by unrighteousness, his upper rooms by injustice, making his countrymen work for nothing, not paying them for their labor. He says, 'I will build myself a great palace with spacious upper rooms.' So he makes large windows in it, panels it with cedar and decorates it in red.

"Does it make you a king to have more and more cedar? Did not your father have food and drink? He did what was right and just, so all went well with him. He defended the cause of the poor and needy, and so all went well. Is that not what it means to know me?" declares the LORD. "But your eyes and your heart are set only on dishonest gain, on shedding innocent blood and on oppression and extortion." . . .

"I warned you when you felt secure, but you said, "I will not listen!" This has been your way from your youth; you have not obeyed me. The wind will drive all your shepherds away, and your allies will go into exile. . . . How you will groan when pangs come upon you, pain like that of a woman in labor."

—Jeremiah 22:13-17, 21-23

By the time Jeremiah spoke these words, King Josiah had been killed in battle with Neco, king of Egypt. In the wake of Josiah's death, Jeremiah grieved this child king who was crowned at the age of eight and led a spiritual renewal in Judah following decades of idolatry and wickedness. While Josiah set in motion reforms that would guide God's people for the next three decades, his death triggered the judgment that Jeremiah had been prophesying—a judgment withheld while Josiah was king. Josiah's son Jehoahaz followed his father to the throne, but within three months was overthrown by Egypt. The Egyptian king replaced him with Jehoiakim, who after an eleven-year reign, characterized by evil and unrighteousness, was carried off to Babylon by King Nebuchadnezzar.

In the passage above, Jeremiah speaks first to Jehoahaz and then to Jehoiakim about their wickedness—manifested in wealth and security obtained at the expense of the poor and needy of Judah. In turning from Yahweh, these kings had embraced other gods, abandoned those on the margins of their society, accumulated wealth unjustly, and sought security in unholy alliances with foreign kings. In mocking rebuke, Jeremiah asks, "Does it make you a king to have more and more cedar?"

Jeremiah's question stings us still: Does it make us better parents if we build bigger houses for our children? Does it make us wiser to have ever more education? Does it make us secure to hoard our wealth in stocks and bonds? Are we happier for spending excessive amounts of money in leisure and recreation? Are we safer by living in gated communities and homes with security systems? Are we smarter by owning the latest high-tech gadgets?

Lessons from Jeremiah about Idolatry

While we may not bow down to idols of stone or wood today, it is clear that we dilute our allegiance to God as much as did the people of God in Jeremiah's day. Anything that weakens our commitment to God and to God's agenda is idolatry, and Jeremiah makes several points about idolatrous lifestyles.

- First, *abandoning Yahweh always leads to idolatry*. We were born to worship something or someone, and when it is no longer Yahweh, it will be almost anything.
- Second, *we become what we worship*. If we worship God, we become like God—holy, just, righteous, compassionate, and more. When we worship anything else we take on its qualities and characteristics as well.
- Third, when we abandon God, *we forsake the very source of our life*. All of our work and effort will gain us nothing without God. While digging for water we will find only dry wells.
- Fourth, when we leave God, *we always create alliances that oppose God and that compromise our identity* as God's people.
- Fifth, when we worship anything besides God, we

inevitably *abandon those on the margins of society.* We begin to accumulate wealth, status, and power without concern for justice. Jeremiah, as did Old Testament prophets before and after him, consistently connected obedience and faithfulness to Yahweh with justice and equity for people on the margins of society—those disregarded and discriminated against by others. Our willingness "to do justice and to love to mercy" is a barometer of the quality of our relationship with God. Failing to care for those on the margins is a sign that we no longer care for Yahweh.

In Jeremiah's day, God's people had abandoned God's policy of jubilee, in which economic equity and justice were to regularly characterize relationships and commercial enterprise. While proclaiming "Peace, peace," they denied their own wounds and sickness (Jeremiah 8:11). Jeremiah described it this way:

Like cages full of birds, their houses are full of deceit; they have become rich and powerful and have grown fat and sleek. . . . They do not plead the case of the fatherless to win it, they do not defend the rights of the poor. (5:27-28)

Preoccupied with Homeland Security

In moving further from God, the people of Judah became increasingly concerned about their own safety, security, and comfort. In language that rings true of Americans since September 11, 2001, they became more and more focused on "homeland security." American anxieties about security are strikingly similar to the concerns of God's people in Jeremiah's day.

But increased rhetoric about protecting national interests—regardless of the costs to others—has had more implications for those on the margins of our society than for the rest of us. In 2006, a number of foreign delegates to Mennonite World Conference in Pasadena, California, were denied visas because of new restrictions placed on visitors to the United States, making it possible that Mennonites will never again be able to have a global gathering here. Anxiety about homeland security has fueled anger against immigrants, particularly Latino/Hispanics. Members of Mennonite congregations in the United States, as far north as Pennsylvania, have been arrested secretly in the night and returned to Mexico, their families left behind without a father or husband to care for them. Members of one Hispanic Mennonite congregation in Pennsylvania arrived one day to find their church building painted with racist graffiti.

Professing Christians have joined this anti-immigration response, failing to recognize the movement of God's Spirit in bringing a world in need of Christ to our very doorsteps. Too often as Christians our interests are those of the rich and powerful, perhaps because, relative to the rest of the world, that is exactly what we are. Our primary concern is about protecting our own wealth, status, power, and position rather than about abandoning all we have to follow Jesus Christ. Concern about homeland security is both a source of our idolatry and a symptom.

But homeland security was an issue among Mennonites long before September 11. Many of our Mennonite ancestors settled in North America largely because it represented a secure, safe place to worship and raise their children, tired as they were of running from their persecutors. Once settled in North America, it did not take us long to forget our foreigner and alien status, to forget the cost of following Jesus in a homeland that had greater security. And since then, we have invested much of our energies on retaining that security, making sure that we remain safe and settled as the "quiet in the land."

Of all people, given our history of persecution and our theology of following Jesus in daily life, Mennonites should be the last to be preoccupied with homeland security. Of all Reformation traditions, we should remember what it is to be the stranger and the alien. But in his history of Lancaster Mennonite Conference, *The Earth Is the Lord's*, John Ruth reports few writings about religious faith and spirituality in Mennonite records from the nineteenth century. Instead, diaries and writings tended to focus on the material things that people were passing down to their children, on business transactions, and so on. Once settled in this country, Mennonites stopped running, and when we did so, we began investing heavily in our own comfort, status, and security.[1]

Jesus made it very clear when he sent seventy-two disciples (Luke 10) to proclaim the kingdom that homeland security was to be the least of their worries. Those who are sent by Jesus must give up their security, and those who fail to do so will likely never begin the journey. If God's people are going to be faithful in proclaiming the good news of Jesus Christ in our homes, across the street, and around the world, we will do so only as we give up our primary commitment to homeland security.

This chapter looks at findings from Mennonite Member Profile 2006 related to the struggles of Mennonites with "homeland security." Mennonites in the United States live in a nation that is the most affluent and powerful of any in history and that has achieved near "empire" status in the world. Living faithfully as followers of Jesus Christ in an empire will require more of us than most of us have given up to this point, and perhaps more than most us will ever be willing to give up.

The Money We Make—And Give Away

Mennonites in North America today are wealthier than Mennonites anywhere else in the world and at any other time in history. Today 20% of Mennonites possess 88% of all the wealth of Mennonites globally. Seven percent of Mennonite households in the United State earned less than $15,000 in 2005. Fifty-three percent earned $50,000 or more and 16% earned more than $100,000. The median household income for Mennonites was $50,000-74,999.

Among Racial/Ethnic members, 18% of households report earning less than $15,000 in 2005, and nearly two-thirds (63%) less than $50,000. Eight percent earned more than $100,000 annually. The median income category among Racial/Ethnic members is $25,000-39,000.

But Mennonites, while affluent, also show signs of strong giving to their churches and to charities. Sixty-one percent of members report giving 10% or more of their household income to church and charitable causes, with 27% giving 11% or more.

Table 6.1	Household income	
	2006	**Racial/Ethnic**
Under $15,000	7	18
$15,000 to $24,999	9	15
$25,000 to $49,999	30	30
$50,000 to $74,999	25	18
$75,000 to $99,999	13	12
$100,000 to $199,999	12	7
More than $200,000	4	1
	Percent	

Members report giving nearly $300 per month in congregational offerings. And 41% of members say that household giving to their local congregation has increased over the past two years, with only 10% saying that it has decreased.

Among other American Christians, however, financial giving is declining. In 1968, evangelicals on average gave 6.2% of their income but by 2001 were giving only 4.3%. Another study showed that in 2002 only 6% of born-again Christians tithed.[2] As American affluence has increased, giving has declined. Reflecting on the imbalance between American wealth and giving, Ron Sider notes:

> American Christians live in the richest nation on earth. . . . If Americans just tithed, they would have another $143 billion available to empower the poor and spread the gospel . . . an additional $70-80 billion a year would be enough to provide access to essential services like healthcare and education for all the poor of the earth. If they did no more than tithe, American Christians would have the private dollars to foot this entire bill and still have $60-70 billion more to do evangelism around the world.[3]

Whether Mennonites—who have become increasingly assimilated into the larger culture—will retain their high levels of giving and funnel their money toward programs that address the inequities experienced by Mennonite brothers and sisters around the world remains to be seen.

The Homes We Keep

Eighty-six percent of Mennonites own their own homes, higher than the national average of 69%. This is slightly higher than in 1972 (80%) and much higher than among Racial/Ethnic Mennonites (65%).[4]

The median home market value among Mennonites is between $150,000 and $199,000, though one-third (34%) of Mennonite homeowners estimate their home to be worth $200,000 or more, and 15% live in homes that are worth more than $300,000.

The Stuff We Own

Mennonites were asked a number of questions about the things they own. We learned the following:

- Ninety-seven percent of Mennonite households have at least one television and nearly two-thirds (62%) have two or more. Thirty percent have three or more televisions, and 10% have four or more. In 1972, 17% of Mennonite households had no television and only 23% had two or more.
- Eighty-one percent of Mennonite households have at least one cell phone—44% have two or more.
- Fourteen percent of Mennonite households have at least one handgun, and 37% have at least one hunting rifle. Among conservative Protestants in the United States, 56% of men have a gun in their home.[5]
- Thirteen percent of Mennonite households have at least one large-screen television.
- Seventy-eight percent of Mennonite households have at least one personal computer.
- Twenty-eight percent of Mennonite households have a video game system.
- Ninety-six percent of households have at least one automobile; more than two thirds (69%) have two or more automobiles; 26% have three or more vehicles, and 10% have four or more vehicles.
- Four percent of Mennonite households have a motor home.

- Seventy-three percent of Mennonites have an Internet connection, 37% a high-speed connection.

Racial/Ethnic Mennonites differ from other Mennonites in some areas of ownership. Half as many (7%) own handguns, and only 11% own hunting rifles. More Racial/Ethnic members own large-screen TVs (22%) than do Anglos, but fewer Racial/Ethnic members own a computer (71%) than do Anglos. More own video game systems (40%), but fewer own vehicles (85%). Only 54% of Racial/Ethnic members are connected to the Internet, 27% with a high-speed connection.

The Security We Create

Mennonites were not always supporters of life, health, and property insurance; for many it was seen as a lack of trust in God. It appears that this struggle of conscience is over, with most Mennonites having multiple types of insurance coverage (though Racial/Ethnic members are less well insured).

- Ninety-four percent of members have some form of health insurance, compared to the national average of 84% who have coverage. Sixteen percent of Racial/Ethnic Mennonites lack healthcare coverage, equal to the national average.
- Eighty-four percent of Mennonites have some form of prescription drug coverage (75% of Racial/Ethnic members).
- Seventy-nine percent of Mennonites have life insurance compared to 69% of Racial/Ethnic members.
- Eighty percent of Mennonites have annuity/retirement plans compared to 69% of Racial/Ethnic members.

The Margins Whites Ignore

In Jeremiah's day, the more God's people focused on themselves and their own security, the more they ignored the poor, the fatherless, and all who were on the margins of their society. As a historically white denomination with a growing proportion of Racial/Ethnic members, Mennonites have still not overcome the substantial boundaries that separate white middle-class members from Racial/Ethnic members, who are often marginalized in both the church and society. Finding ways to authentically eliminate the

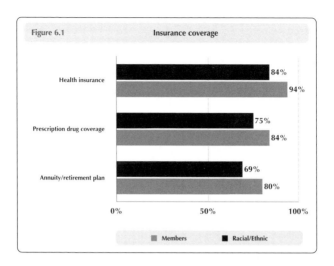

Figure 6.1 — Insurance coverage

Health insurance — Members 94%, Racial/Ethnic 84%
Prescription drug coverage — Members 84%, Racial/Ethnic 75%
Annuity/retirement plan — Members 80%, Racial/Ethnic 69%

Members | Racial/Ethnic

intentional efforts by those in the middle of the church—those with power, affluence, and status.

In my view, the failure of white Mennonites to actively overcome the remnants of historic racism is one sign of our idolatry. The early church clearly prioritized caring for those on the margins, as described by early Christian apologist Aristides:

> They walk in all humility and kindness, and falsehood is not found among them, and they love one another. They despise not the widow, and grieve not the orphan. He that hath, distributeth liberally to him that hath not. If they see a stranger they bring him under their roof, and rejoice over him. . . . And if there is among them a man that is poor and needy, and they have not an abundance . . . they fast two or three days that may supply the needy with their necessary food.[6]

Michael Emerson, evangelical sociologist at Rice University, along with his colleagues, has done some of the best work on the issue of racism among evangelicals in the U.S. They suggest:

> While there have been notable exceptions, most congregations [in the United States] have not been places of racial shalom. There is a stark contrast between the first-century church and Christian congregations in the United States.

> The impact of racism on Christianity in the United States, from colonial times to the present, has produced a religion in which most congregations are uniracial. The racial division of congregations has become a defining characteristic of the Christian faith in the United States. . . . Congregations in the United States, in most cases, have failed to embrace the New Testament theology of oneness and practice of multiracial assemblies. Racism is a sin and a racially divided church does not reflect Jesus' vision of a house of prayer for all the nations.[7]

Among Racial/Ethnic Mennonites in Mennonite Church USA, 14% report they have been unfairly treated because of their race or ethnicity by other Mennonites. Forty percent of Mennonite Racial/Ethnic ministers state that they have felt unfairly treated for the same reasons.

In conversations with Racial/Ethnic pastors and members during this study, I heard deep frustration with a church that seems to be ignoring those on its margins. Comments included:

- Mennonites only come to our churches when they want to conduct research projects or to do missions. They should evangelize and serve their own neighborhoods before trying to do so in our communities.
- Mennonites make promises but too often don't keep them.
- There is a table where white Mennonites are making decisions and resources are allocated, but Racial/Ethnic persons aren't at that table.
- Sometimes our refusal to participate in church-related activities is related to the fact that the only power we feel we have is the power to say no.

Given the essence of what Racial/Ethnic pastors and members feel about their place among other Mennonites, it is not surprising that Racial/Ethnic members are more likely than other Mennonites to support intentional efforts in both the church and larger society to overcome racism and discrimination.

Fifty percent of Racial/Ethnic members believe that it is very important that leaders and staff of church-related agencies reflect the Racial/Ethnic diversity of Mennonite congregations. This compares with only 26% of Anglo Mennonites. Twenty-eight percent of

Racial/Ethnic members strongly support intentional efforts to hire and promote Racial/Ethnic minorities in the larger society compared to 4% of white Mennonite who strongly support such efforts. Thirty-nine percent of Racial/Ethnic members believe that it is very important that church leaders address issues of race and racism, compared to 27% of white Mennonites who believe the same.

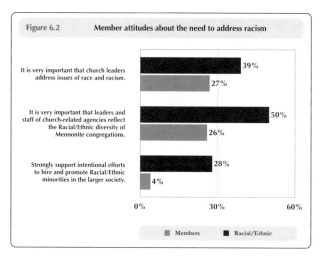

Figure 6.2   Member attitudes about the need to address racism

The leadership of Mennonite Church USA has recognized the challenge that the church faces, making anti-racism one of the four priorities of the denomination. But while denominational leaders may call the church to pay attention to those on the margins, members are clearly not as committed to the issue. My own sense is that many white Mennonites have little awareness of the number of Racial/Ethnic members who are part of Mennonite Church USA. In addition, few whites in North America are sensitive to issues of race or aware of how racism is both intentionally and unintentionally perpetuated within the church. A major form of such racism is "institutional racism," in which discriminatory policies and decisions are often made unintentionally but with the same results as intentional discrimination. Examples include the exclusion or absence of Racial/Ethnic members in decision-mak-

exclusion or absence of Racial/Ethnic members in decision-making processes, social networks that fail to include Racial/Ethnic persons and in which significant decisions are often made informally, and opportunities for which Racial/Ethnic members are given little consideration.

Prior to my own involvement with Mennonite Member Profile 2006, I too lived with little awareness of the number of Racial/Ethnic members in Mennonite Church USA or of the barriers that existed to their greater involvement and integration in the church (despite my experiences as both a pastor in the denomination and as a sociologist who teaches about race and ethnicity). The challenge for congregations, area conferences, and the denomination is to create opportunities for worship, service, and relationships that intentionally cross racial and ethnic lines. If we simply wait for this to occur it never will.

When asked about the changes needed in the church to overcome racism and barriers that confront Racial/Ethnic members and congregations, one Racial/Ethnic pastor noted that the changes would need to be structural, cultural, and economic: "I think the Mennonite church as a system would begin to embrace and truly bring about an appreciation that would prompt it to begin to change how it does church—how it makes decisions, how it distributes resources, and how it places individuals in positions."

Too often the response of white persons to concerns about racism are along the following lines:

- Racial/Ethnic members do not want to be "tokens," and so we should not intentionally invite them to participate or serve with us.
- Diversity should be about more than race and gender. After all, lots of people feel marginalized—why favor women and persons of color?
- Diversity is about bringing together the greatest minds and most creative talent, so focusing on gender or racial diversity is shortsighted. Instead we should focus on all types of diversity.
- Race doesn't matter anymore. Christians should be beyond conversations about race; there are no racial differences in God's family.

While each of these points warrants further discussion, these responses tend to come from those in the majority rather than in the minority. Such comments shut down further conversation about the injustices and inequities felt by Racial/Ethnic brothers and sisters. And too often, such conversations occur without Racial/Ethnic members at the table, with too few of them attending gatherings, serving on committees, and sharing in the church's resources. Diversity in the church is not primarily about bringing the most creative minds to the same table; it is about addressing the sins of injustice and inequity in which whites have historically participated, including white Mennonites. It is about eliminating the differences between margin and middle that are too often determined, even today, by race and ethnicity.

Part of the challenge of this kind of conversation is that racial issues in the United States have become defined as political issues—race has become politicized. Political polarization among Mennonites has intensified differences around issues of racism and discrimination in the church. In 1972, the member profile asked six questions about race, different than those asked in 2006. While the results of the 1972 survey revealed a level of prejudice among Mennonites, only one of the questions showed any significant difference between Republicans and Democrats. In other words, attitudes about race were no different regardless of one's political affiliation.

Table 6.2	Differences in attitudes about racism by political identity		
		Republicans	Democrats
Believe it is very important that leaders and staff of church-related agencies reflect the Racial/Ethnic diversity across Mennonite congregations.		21	41
Strongly support intentional efforts to hire and promote Racial/Ethnic minorities to overcome patterns of racism in our society.		3	13
Believe it is very important that church leaders discuss and address issues of race and racism.		20	43
Believe that immigration is a "very good thing."		7	26
		Percent	

In Mennonite Member Profile 2006, the differences between Republicans and Democrats on questions of race and racism are statistically significant in every case, with Republicans consistently less supportive of efforts to address racism than Democrats.

Scripture affirms in both Old and New Testaments that there is no room in God's kingdom for differences based on race and ethnicity. Yet like the Jerusalem church in the first century, situated as it was in the "middle" with "majority" power, Mennonites in the middle and the majority have also failed to extend full fellowship to Racial/Ethnic brothers and sisters.

The Presidents We Elect

The increased politicization of Mennonites today was seen in a number of ways in the Mennonite Member Profile 2006. In 1972, 66% disagreed with the statement that "Mennonites should not vote in national elections." Today 93% of members believe that Mennonites should vote. For at least thirty-five years, Mennonites have been more Republican than Democrat, though both political parties have gained adherents over that time period.

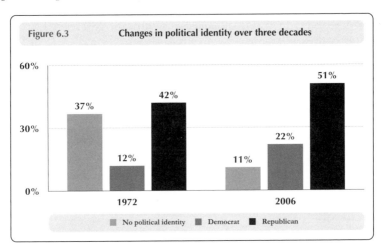

Figure 6.3   Changes in political identity over three decades

Today 51% of Mennonites identify with the Republican Party, compared to 42% in 1972. Twenty-two percent identify as Democrats, compared to 12% in 1972. The proportion of Independents and others has increase from 10% thirty-five years ago to 16% today. In sum, the percentage who did not identify with any political party has dropped from 37% in 1972 to only 11% today. Of Mennonites who voted in the last 2004 election, two-thirds supported George W. Bush.

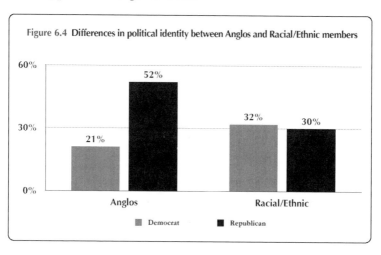

Figure 6.4 Differences in political identity between Anglos and Racial/Ethnic members

Racial/Ethnic members are less likely to identify with a political party than other Mennonites, with 27% claiming no political party in contrast to just 11% of Anglos. However, this difference is in large part due to the immigrant status of many Racial/Ethnic members: 38% of immigrants do not identify with a political party, compared to 16% among those born in the United States. Racial/Ethnic members who do identify with a political party are slightly more likely to be Democrat (32%) than Republican (30%), compared with Anglo Mennonites who are more likely to be Republican (52%) than Democrat (21%). Mennonites are more Republican than both conservative Protestants and mainline Protestants in the United States. Conservative Protestants are 36% Republican whereas mainline Protestants are 37% Republican.[8]

Among African-Americans nationally, just 6% are Republican. Greeley and Hout, in their national study of Americans, found that while African-Americans are evangelical in their beliefs, they are more likely to vote Democratic than non-evangelicals. This finding parallels what we see about Racial/Ethnic Mennonites. Though as a group they are just as evangelical in their beliefs as other Mennonites (even more so), they are as likely to vote Democrat as Republican.

In explaining how evangelical beliefs can lead to very different political party affiliations, Greeley and Hout note:

> Literal interpretation of the Bible and frequent religious practice push African-Americans toward the Democrats and whites toward the Republicans. . . . To put the matter differently, the gospel does correlate with political orientation; the direction of the correlation depends on believers' social contexts, which in this case means their differing racial ancestries.[9]

Among Mennonites, a similar pattern exists. Racial/Ethnic members, who are even more likely to identify as "evangelical" than are other Mennonites, are no more likely to be Republican than Democrat. While Americans frequently identify Christianity with Republican and right-wing politics, Racial/Ethnic members do not. Instead Racial/Ethnic members, with greater concerns for social justice and for those on the margins, are equally likely to embrace the socially progressive platform of Democrats as the conservative agenda of Republicans. Racial/Ethnic Christians reveal that one can be a committed evangelical, even Pentecostal/charismatic, and be politically to the left of center as well. Interestingly, Greeley and Hout also found that all Pentecostals, including whites, were more likely to vote Democratic than Republican, despite the fact that Pentecostals were by almost all measures of evangelicalism (beliefs, practices, and evangelism) more devout than even Protestant evangelicals. Greeley and Hout conclude:

> Conservative Christianity in both its American forms constitutes a single powerful religious story—God is on the side of his people as they struggle for freedom. In their own way the conservative Protestants and the Afro-American Protestants identify with that story and bestow their alle-

giance of party loyalty to the party that best reflects that collective self-image.[10]

The Nation We Protect

For being a people whose history began with a rejection of national security, Mennonites are increasingly embracing this security. Fifty-six percent believe it is "all right for Christians to be in noncombatant service in the armed forces." Only twenty-three percent believe that it is "always wrong" to enter the armed forces, and only 5% believe it is "always wrong" to work as a police officer.

Twenty-one percent would enter the military if faced with a draft, another 10% are unsure about what they would do, and 65% would choose alternative service as a conscientious objector. In 1972, 11% of Mennonites said they would have chosen military service and 5% were unsure, while 81% would choose alternative service as a conscientious objector. By 1989 the percentage that would enter military service had increased to 16%, and those who would choose alternative service declined slightly to 77%. The change in this response is greater between 1989 and 2006 than between 1972 and 1989, again suggesting the more rapid recent assimilation of Mennonites into the broader American culture and political life of the nation. In addition,

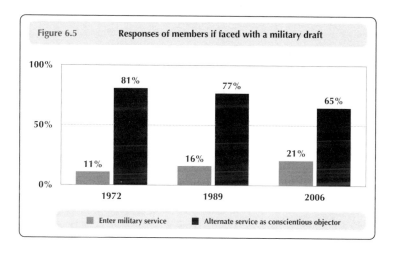

Figure 6.5   Responses of members if faced with a military draft

while 27% of members agreed that a Christian could file a lawsuit in 1972, 43% agree today. And while 30% were comfortable swearing an oath in 1972, 46% are today.

Despite these changes that show more willingness to support military service, Mennonites still show a substantial commitment to the ideals of peacemaking. Seventy-one percent agree that "all war is sin" and 65% that it is "wrong for Christians to fight in any war." Eighty-five percent agree that "complete nonviolence as a way of living is very important to me." Ninety-three percent of members believe that "peacemaking is a central theme of the gospel."

At the same time, many Mennonites appear to have more fully embraced a national identity and their citizenship within that nation. Almost half of Mennonites (48%) believe that America is a Christian nation; 67% would pledge allegiance to the flag, and more than one-third (35%) believe it is okay to fly an American flag inside a Mennonite church. Nearly 25% support the war in Iraq, and 42% believe that the "war on terror" is a religious battle.

The increased importance of political identity among Mennonites threatens to take priority over our theological and spiritual identity. In this vein, I once heard a Mennonite pastor reflect his unwillingness to consider a number of social issues that were being discussed out of

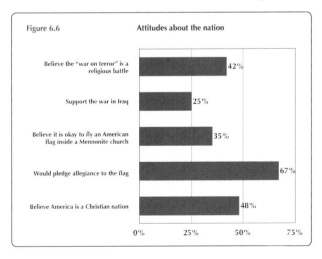

Figure 6.6   Attitudes about the nation

fear that in doing so he would "become a Democrat." This trumping of theology by politics is one of the motivations for John D. Roth's argument for a "sabbatical" from party politics among Mennonites in order to "develop a shared language for political witness that is rooted clearly and unmistakably within the framework of the church and our prior, primary allegiance to Jesus and the gospel."[11] But for better or worse, members who responded to Mennonite Member Profile 2006 appear to soundly reject any such notion. The challenge for Mennonites, who are more politically engaged today and who lean more Republican than Democrat, is to retain our historic commitment to the separation of church and state and a commitment to follow the way of Jesus in loving our enemies and responding nonviolently in all areas of life. The evidence suggests that we are being pulled toward an allegiance to the nation that is becoming more important than our allegiance to Jesus Christ.

In reflecting upon this temptation for conservative Protestants in the United States, Greeley and Hout note:

> Conservative Protestants have more national pride than other Americans and feel more strongly than people of other religions that the rest of the world ought to imitate the United States. . . . While there is no harm in rooting for sports teams or even touting one's standard of living or achievements in culture and science, other countries could have cause to worry if the source of pride falls closer to the militaristic and historical roots associated with rampant nationalism. And that, for the most part, is where the distinctive pride of conservative Protestants lies. . . . Conservative Protestants are conspicuously patriotic. Their members are prominent in the military and at public events that have a patriotic flavor. They express more pride, especially in the military, than other Americans do.[12]

As Mennonites have become more Republican and more ready to embrace a national citizenship, we have become less likely to resist military service and more likely to say that we would engage in war or carry a weapon. This tendency will likely continue unless there are major changes in Mennonite political identity or we simply withdraw from politics. It is possible, like other denominations that began with peacemaking commitments (e.g. Assemblies of God, Seventh Day Adventists), Mennonites may eventually abandon the radical peace-making nature of the gospel.

The Home We Have Forgotten

Some have observed that Christians talk less about heaven today than in the past. While this may be true, 95% of Men-nonites still believe that there "is life after death" and 90% that "there is a real heaven where some people are eternally rewarded." Mennonites are less certain about hell, with 78% believing that there is a "real hell where people are eternally punished." But when asked about their views of Jesus, only 43% noted that they "eagerly anticipated Jesus' return to earth." Among other Americans, 87% of conservative Protestants believe in an afterlife, 81% of African-Americans, and 86% of mainline Protestants.[13]

Conclusion

A focus on homeland security is antithetical to all that Jesus taught his disciples about the cost of following him. When Jesus sent out the seventy-two disciples in Luke 10, he instructed them to carry neither purse nor bag nor sandals—nothing that they needed to feel secure; maybe not even what they thought they needed to do what Jesus had commanded. But giving up our purses, bags, and sandals is going to be a big problem for many Mennonites if we are going to respond faithfully to Jesus' call, because for many of us, there will be a lot to give up.

There is ample discussion among Mennonites today about Anabaptist identity. While I affirm the discussion, I think it has less to do with our failure to understand what Jesus requires than our failure to carry out what we already know is required of Christ's disciples. I suspect that if we were more faithful in being sent into the world, the problem of identity would take care of itself. We would soon become known as those with no purse, no bag, and no shoes and those who willingly embraced the alien and the orphan. While it did not take long for our European ancestors to develop an identity as pilgrims and strangers, it has been harder for their descendants in North America to live back into that identity.

Mennonites need once again to embrace a theology that acknowledges we are strangers and foreigners and that accepts our alien status, not by being the "quiet in the land" but by boldly and willingly being sent into a dying world in the name of our Lord. As we pitch our tents alongside other strangers and aliens, we will eliminate the boundaries that exist between liberals and conservatives, evangelicals and Anabaptists, as well as those in Mennonite Church USA and those outside it, and others. Such boundaries are artificial and have little to do with being the church of Christ. These boundaries have been established and maintained by those of us with too much time on our hands—too much time at home trying to keep things neat and secure, guarding the gates of our homeland.

One pastor in the eastern United States who formerly lived in the West frequently laments the failure of Mennonites of different streams in the East to worship and serve together as they do where he came from. Because there are fewer of them living in what could hardly be considered a "Mennonite heartland," I suspect western Mennonites are better at seeing what they have in common than in looking for what divides them. I would never wish on Mennonite Church USA the same outcome as the tower of Babel, but I am not sure some dispersion from our comfortable centers would hurt us. In fact, it might be the answer to the conflicts that we have faced in becoming too comfortable where we are.

I also fear that as parents and grandparents we have burdened our children with our homeland worries rather than encouraging them to hear the voice of God sending them into the world. While encouraging them to be respectable, professional, honorable, and wise, we have given them the same message that the world gives about success. Too rarely do we challenge them to consider the rewards of being sent into the world for the sake of the kingdom.

Many of us want our children at home, especially since we're having fewer of them. While we look with disgust at the way the people of Israel sometimes sacrificed their own children to idols, I wonder if we've not done the same at times. We may not sacrifice our children to Molech, but what about to Main Street or Wall Street? We may not send our young men and women to war in Iraq, but would we allow them to go there if they felt called to join Christian Peacemaker Teams? Or what if they wanted to be missionaries to the Sudan or Turkey or Somalia? Would we bless them in going and celebrate their answer to God's call? Or if they initiated a Bible study in our community, using our home? Or if they began to develop new ideas for evangelism and social action in our congregations? Would we support them? Would we allow them to try? Could the adults get out of the way long enough to see if they could pull it off?

If we are ever going to be obedient to God's missional call, we must come to terms with our insecurities and, frankly, our idols—to come to a point of being willing to give up everything and everyone we hold dear. But why should that surprise us, given Jesus' words about gaining the world and losing our souls?

As the Mennonite Member Profile 2006 data shows, Racial/Ethnic members are poorer, less likely to own their home, and less likely to have health insurance than white Mennonites. God's message through the Old Testament prophets was consistently a message about caring for those on the margins—for the poor, the fatherless, the widows. Doing so was a barometer of spirituality for God's people. Whenever they wandered away from God, they also wandered away from those on the margins. Why? Because the poor and discriminated against simply are not strategically important to those who are in the middle accumulating wealth, status, and power. It is only in relationship with God that God's people ever reach out to the margins.

There are substantial barriers today between Racial/Ethnic members and white Mennonites. Social, economic, cultural, geographic, historical, residential, and language differences are too often maintained rather than challenged, and in the process remain barriers to the development of meaningful relationships and collaboration across racial and ethnic lines.

Questions that remain for the church to struggle with include: Can white Mennonites give up their wealth, power, prestige, and status to partner with Racial/Ethnic Mennonites? Can both groups of Mennonites find unity in things that should concern us all, such as peacemaking, social justice, and personal transformation through Jesus Christ? Can the margins be eliminated? Can homeland security become a thing of the past? Can we be faithful in being sent into the world?

7

587 BC—The Fall

Therefore the LORD Almighty says this: "Because you have not listened to my words, I will summon all the peoples of the north and my servant Nebuchadnezzar king of Babylon . . . and I will bring them against this land and its inhabitants and against all the surrounding nations. I will completely destroy them and make them an object of horror and scorn, and an everlasting ruin. I will banish from them the sounds of joy and gladness, the voices of bride and bridegroom. . . . This whole country will become a desolate wasteland, and these nations will serve the king of Babylon seventy years."—Jeremiah 25:8-11

On the tenth day of the fifth month, in the nineteenth year of Nebuchadnezzar king of Babylon, Nebuzaradan commander of the imperial guard, who served the king of Babylon, came to Jerusalem. He set fire to the temple of the LORD, the royal palace and all the houses of Jerusalem. Every important building he burned down. The whole Babylonian army under the commander of the imperial guard broke down all the walls around Jerusalem. . . . The Babylonians broke up the bronze pillars, the movable stands and the bronze Sea that were at the temple of the LORD and they carried all the bronze to Babylon. They also took away the pots, shovels, wick trimmers, sprinkling bowls, dishes and all the bronze articles . . . the basins, censers, sprinkling bowls, pots, lampstands, dishes and bowls used for drink offerings. . . . So Judah went into captivity, away from her land.
—Jeremiah 52:12-15, 17-19, 27

In 587 BC, all of the doom and gloom that Jeremiah had been prophesying for decades came to pass. God's words proved true, despite assurances to the contrary by false prophets and reassuring priests. King Nebuchadnezzar and his sidekick, Nebuzaradan, successfully did what God had anointed them to do—they delivered judgment to a guilty people.

But even the prophet Jeremiah, despite years of prophesying this catastrophe, seemed unable to get his mind around the desecration and destruction of Jerusalem, and particularly of the temple. He lingered over the inventory of temple artifacts removed by Nebuchadnezzar's imperial guard. One can almost hear him saying, "I just can't quite believe it—even the wick trimmers off to Babylon!" But God had accomplished what God had promised, using Judah's enemy to the north to create seventy years of quiet and rest for a land long characterized by idolatry and disobedience.

Denying Death and Disruption

Besides their idolatry—or perhaps because of their idolatry—God's people lived in continual denial of God's reality. They were unable and unwilling to accept the imminent destruction of Jerusalem and the temple by Nebuchadnezzar. Rather than placing their confidence in God, they trusted in the familiarity of their religious practices, the sacredness of their identity as God's people, and the security of holy places such as the temple. Jeremiah warned that these things were sacred only as long as they were part of a relationship with Yahweh. Aside from that, nothing was holy except in the people's own minds. God's judgment destroyed all that the people had considered sacred in order that they might once again worship Yahweh alone and accept his reality.

But who can blame God's people for their resistance to Jeremiah's message that all they held sacred was going to be destroyed? Who of us is willing to accept the disruption and death of those things that we hold most dear—our religious practices, our religious identity, and the church buildings we cherish? This difficulty is painfully clear when congregations shrink to just a few faithful attendees. Efforts to revitalize such congregations are usually unsuccessful unless those who remain are willing to acknowledge the death of what they knew and allow God's Spirit to create a new future for them.

In *Off-Road Disciplines: Spiritual Adventures of Missional Leaders*, Earl Creps tells the story of the Lutheran congregation in which he grew up and of which his father was pastor. A robust congregation with two services in the 1960s, the church built a large educational complex and gymnasium to enhance the church's ministry. But just thirty years later, the neighborhood around the congregation had completely changed as white and black middle-class residents fled to the suburbs. The members' responses to the changes, writes Creps, were defensive; they literally locked themselves inside the church building, fortressing themselves against the neighborhood.

> The congregation's unspoken strategy assumed that we could stay in place until our sheer presence wore down both the global economy and local sociology by attrition, bringing a glorious return to the late sixties. It never happened. . . . In the 1990s, I preached at my father's retirement service with a small, white-haired remnant scattered among the many dozens of dark wood pews.[1]

As Mennonites, we have just as much difficulty—and perhaps even more—accepting the disruption and death of our congregations and spiritual realities. A once thriving rural congregation that I know in the eastern United States has transitioned from pastor to pastor for several decades in hopes that each one will bring a new future by revitalizing the congregation, evangelizing the local community, and once again filling the pews. But pastor after pastor exits without such changes, and the same small, dwindling group of faithful saints continues as it has for several decades. Across Mennonite Church USA, congregations and area conferences face disruption and uncertain change, including membership decline.

Why do congregations, area conferences, and denominations—like the people of God in Jeremiah's day—too often refuse to act, even when faced with the facts of their own death and disruption? Perhaps it is for the same reason that individuals refuse to change: lack of courage, little faith in God, confidence in other things, and a denial of reality. Few of us willingly accept the death of that which is most familiar to us, especially when we believe it to be holy and sacred, such as our churches. Maybe it is too much to expect people to come to terms with the destruction of those things that have given meaning during tragedy, brought comfort in sorrow, and provided a stable community in an ever-changing world. Of all places where most of us want stability, it is in our local congregations.

It seems especially difficult for adults and long-time church members to accept change and disruption in our churches. For this reason, the innovations and ideas of youth in the church are resisted. Too often young people hear, "But we've never done it that way before" or "We don't have the money for that" or "You didn't ask for permission." For many of us, history—rather than Scripture, the Spirit, or objective reality—shapes our decisions about what to accept or reject. Perhaps this is why Jesus said that it is the children, not the wise and learned, who will see the kingdom (see Luke 10:21). Perhaps only children have few enough years to accept the possibility that "what is" may not be all that God has in store. Perhaps it is children who have the most pliable hearts and minds to be able to imagine something different. Adulthood for many is the time to calcify our existence against the death that we know is coming.

Living in the "Limen"

I am well aware of my own resistance to accepting the loss of that which is most familiar and of my own anxiety about change in a church that I love and that I believe is part of God's plans and purposes. Yet I also know that it is quite possible that, like you, I have grown to love "churchly" and religious things that God is indeed declaring dead. If the church in North America has any chance of renewal, its members are going to have to accept that much of what we call sacred and holy is now dead, or at least on life support. This renewal will require persons of courage, hope, and imagination who are unafraid of death even while living in the uncertainty of what will be.

Psychologists call this kind of existence "liminal," the root word of which is *limen*, or threshold. To live in liminality is to remain in an "in-between place" that is neither here nor there. Liminality is a place of disequilibrium, where reality has been disrupted and everything seems a bit out of balance. Liminality is where change most often occurs in the lives of individuals and organizations, because in liminal situations the discomfort of uncertainty becomes so intense that change becomes easier to accept.

Liminality is not a place that many of us naturally seek. Sometimes only crisis sends us there. Those who live in earthquake-prone areas know that a doorway (or a limen) is the safest place to be if caught in a building during an earthquake. A doorframe has more support than any other part of a wall. And of course we know from Scripture that it is in this place that we also meet Christ, who says, "I stand at the door and knock" (Revelation 3:20).

In his poem "I Stand at the Door," Samuel Shoemaker describes the liminal experience as well as anyone:

> I stand by the door.
> I neither go too far in, nor stay too far out,
> The door is the most important door in the world—
> It is the door through which men walk when they find God.
> There's no use my going way inside, and staying there.
> When so many are still outside and they, as much as I,
> Crave to know where the door is.
> And all that so many ever find
> Is only a wall where a door ought to be.
> They creep along the wall like blind men,
> Feeling for a door, knowing there must be a door,
> Yet, they never find it . . .
> So I stand by the door.
>
> The people too far in do not see how near these are
> To leaving—preoccupied with the wonder of it all.
> Somebody must watch for those who have entered the door,
> But would like to run away. So for them, too, I stand by the
>   door.
> I admire the people who go way in.
> But I wish they would not forget how it was
> Before they got in. Then they would be able to help
> The people who have not yet even found the door,

> Or the people who want to run away again from God.
> You can go in too deeply, and stay in too long,
> And forget the people outside the door . . .
> So I shall stand by the door and wait
> For those who seek it.
> "I had rather be a door-keeper . . ."
> So I stand by the door.[2]

In this moving poem, Shoemaker articulates the missional calling of individuals and of congregations—to stand in the door, neither fully out nor fully in, but waiting for those who have not yet entered God's house. This is certainly an uncomfortable place to be, full of insecurities and uncertainty.

In fact, missional theologians frequently refer to the current predicament of the church as one of liminality. We live in a period of disequilibrium between the old Christendom of yesterday and the new future of God's reign. Living in liminality is anxiety producing, and the temptation is to go back to where we came from and back to who we were. But the only way that the church will be motivated to fulfill its missional calling is to "stay in the limen." As missional theologian and pastor Alan Roxburgh writes, "Like the biblical texts of Jeremiah and Isaiah . . . God has brought the western church into an experience of liminality within its own cultural world, a place of marginalization, in order that it might hear again the word of God."[3]

Jeremiah's message to the kings, prophets, and people of Israel and Judah was essentially this: "Stay in the limen! Accept God's judgment. Come to terms with your own death, or it will come to terms with you." But in the end, they could not. And so, death caught up with them. And in the end, for the church in North America, if we do not also come to terms with our present disruption and accept our liminal reality, death will also come to terms with us. But for many of us, it may seem easier to die in denial, clinging to what is dear but false, than to realistically confront our demise in the name of the One who has overcome death and hell. Roxburgh writes:

People look around at churches full of people and it seems to them that these are signs that all is well in the land. Indeed, the assumption is that if there is a problem with a specific congregation or denomination . . . [a]ll that needs to be done is figure out the correct methodology for the moment and recalibrate the system for success just like those other church groups that seem to be thriving at the moment. This is precisely the lie the religious leaders of Jerusalem used against Jeremiah prior to the exile. It was all a matter of finding the right tactics; God was, after all on their side and nothing could change that reality.[4]

The Fall of Christendom

Nearly two decades ago, several theologians and church leaders began to discuss concerns that they heard being raised by Bishop Lesslie Newbigin of Great Britain, a veteran missionary to India who returned to his home country only to find that Western society was in many ways "post-Christian" and even anti-Christian, in contrast to when he had left decades before.[5] Like much of Western society until the mid-twentieth century, England had at one time been firmly embedded in what many have come to call Christendom, or the church of the European West formed around AD 400.[6]

Christendom refers to the fact that in most of Europe and North America, societies for centuries had reflected or at least been influenced by Christian values and vocabulary. Within Christendom, life for most persons was organized around religious activity and relationships. Christianity provided a culture, language, organization, and set of experiences that were at least nominally shared by most in these societies. This reality was reflected in the art, music, and scholarship of European cultures, in the everyday life of village peasants, in the arrangement of most towns around a church or cathedral, and in the theocracies of Europe.

Several historical factors began to change this reality and to weaken Christendom's hold on the West. The Reformation in the fifteenth and sixteenth centuries diminished the power and authority of Roman Catholicism and demolished any notion of "one true faith." The Enlightenment soon followed and challenged the truth of religious assumptions and values, leading to a scientific worldview that questioned previous understandings of God. Ron Sider describes this process:

> For almost fifteen hundred years, Western civilization had been grounded in a shared conviction that God, at the center of reality, was the source of moral norms, governmental authority, truth, and beauty. But in the eighteenth century leading thinkers began to argue that the ever more successful scientific project would make the "hypothesis" of God unnecessary. Nothing exists except the material world described with ever-greater scientific precision. The individual replaced God as the center of reality.[7]

Political revolutions in America and France challenged the authority of theocracies that had assumed God's anointing on kings and rulers. However, daily life for most persons in Europe and North America remained embedded in religious ritual, structure, and values into the early twentieth century.

Rapid technological change in the last century, however, coupled with Enlightenment admiration for empirical knowledge rather than faith, brought radical changes to western societies. Suddenly, societies that had been relatively stable in terms of beliefs, values, and shared experiences underwent substantial change. In the United States, the mass migration of European Catholics and later of persons from all religious backgrounds and nationalities also began to dilute the stability of Christendom. Sociologists typically point to the middle of the twentieth century as that moment when American culture and society was most fundamentally altered by changing technology, increases in education, upward mobility, changing beliefs about race and gender, and other social and cultural forces.

In the midst of all these changes, the church too was changed, along with perceptions of the church. The authority and high esteem that the church and its leaders had typically enjoyed across American society diminished. Where the church had once been the center of rural communities and small towns, it was now replaced by educational institutions and entertainment venues (sports, movies, travel).

Where relationships had once been nurtured in the context of community and congregational life, relationships became less stable and predictable with increased mobility and competition from other social institutions. While the church could once depend on the loyalty of its members for support, members now found themselves in a religious marketplace where they could shop from church to church, looking for the right mix of product, privilege, and opportunity. And among Mennonites, where church leaders were called by God (manifested in the "lot") and served their congregation for a lifetime, leaders were now paid professionals whose length of term was annually reevaluated and who were hired and fired by congregational vote.

The result of all this was that western culture changed dramatically during the last century and with it, the church. The church that we knew and loved and found comfort in has fallen into hard times. In this new world, church members are individualistic and disloyal consumers, skeptical of religious organizations and leaders. In missional language, all of these forces brought about the death of Christendom.

Resistance to the Missional Message

Like the message of Jeremiah, the missional discussion has faced much criticism in the church, often over the very word itself. Repeatedly one hears, "But that word is not in the dictionary," suggesting that the only reality worth anything is that which can be found in encyclopedias, dictionaries, and other reference books! This kind of insistence on standardized definitions is exactly the kind of resistance that Jeremiah faced. The absence of a dictionary definition of "missional" does not preclude the reality of its presence in the Scripture or in God's reality. In the end, those who are willing to acknowledge the disruption and crisis in the church will find themselves turning less to rational and formal definitions of reality and more to the living words of God through Scripture and the Spirit.

Resistance to the sociological realities and theological promises of a missional message reflects the fact that most of us have difficulty not only accepting new words, but even more the realities that lie behind those words. Reuben Corrasco, Mennonite pastor and leader in Peru, in describing the movement of God's Spirit among the growing Mennonite churches in Peru, has said, "When God gives a new vision, he gives new language to describe it."

At its core, missional is the following:

1. A sociology that addresses the disruption and decline of Christianity—or Christendom—in Europe and North America, a decline that continues to be ignored by most of us to our peril.

2. A theology to motivate a church wallowing in lethargy and its unwillingness to speak the words of God to the world that "God so loved."

3. A proactive response for local congregations to embrace the reality of Christendom's fall and imagine a new future just as Jeremiah did.

Mennonites and the Disruption of Their Christendom

So far, I have been arguing that Christendom, as reflected in the western Church, has fallen into hard times. But in what ways are Mennonites today experiencing this reality? Are Mennonites different from other Christians in the degree of disruption they are encountering? How are Mennonites dealing with the missional realities of their worlds? This chapter reviews some findings already reported in previous chapters, doing so in the light of the questions I have raised above, while also introducing some new data.

Crisis in membership. In chapter three I reported the membership decline for Mennonite Church USA (and the two earlier denominations it represents: General Conference Mennonite Church and [Old] Mennonite Church) since 1972 as well as its decrease in membership share among Anabaptists nationally and globally. In North America today, there is little growth among Anabaptists except for Old Order and Racial/Ethnic groups. One of the common denominators for both of these is their social and cultural marginality relative to the larger church and society; they are less assimilated in the broader culture. While social and cultural marginality alone does not ensure growth, these groups show that being on the margins does not necessarily inhibit membership growth.

I also noted in chapter three that Mennonites are aging, even ahead of the nation as a whole and some other Christian denominations. The average Mennonite is fifty-four years old, five years older than in 1989. More importantly, the proportion of members in childbearing age is rapidly declining, with only 30% of Mennonites between the ages of eighteen and forty-five, down from 45% in 1989. And the fertility rate of those within childbearing age is only 1.4 children, not nearly the 2.0 children required to sustain population replacement levels.

In describing the membership decline of mainline Protestants, Greeley and Hout report what they might as well have said of Mennonites:

> The mainline Protestants are literally dying out. Slowly but surely they are not only becoming a declining share of the Protestant population but decreasing absolutely. . . . They are, quite simply, failing to reproduce themselves.[8]

These two sociologists argue that birth control is the culprit for a decline that exceeds that of conservative Protestants; birth control and family planning were simply accepted by mainliners earlier than among others. Beyond birth control, it is not as clear why birth rates are so low among Mennonites, except for the possibility of education's negative effect. Demographic research has consistently shown that education negatively affects the number of children one has. The higher-than-national levels of education among Mennonites may help to explain their low levels of fertility. Perhaps Mennonites are educating themselves to death!

The proportion of members under forty-five years of age and low fertility rates predict a continued decline in Mennonite members unless there is an influx of new members. Respondents in Mennonite Member Profile 2006 expressed anxieties about the declines in membership and number of congregations. Some respondents are keenly aware of this crisis and made the following reflections:

• In our small "Mennonite" communities we have gone from nine "Mennonite" churches in the last ten years to five with the "Mennonite" name. And I believe it will only be one with the "Mennonite" name ten years from now. One has closed and another will soon close—the rest are getting smaller.

- One thing I feel and dislike—many older members think if we don't do things like they were fifty years ago that it's wrong—churches are losing members because of that.
- Many of the members who experience a vibrant Christian life leave to go to other churches that they have more in common with.
- I believe our local church is in trouble. Many have left the church and I'm afraid there are no plans to return—they are attending church elsewhere.
- The younger generation (mine)—many end up leaving the church once out of high school and on their own. Is it not "cool" enough to be a Menno? I don't want the church to be obsolete in a hundred years.

Organizational disruption. The merger of the two largest Mennonite denominations unified two faith traditions that shared theological and historical roots. But the decision created a liminal moment—for some who would later leave the new denomination and those refused to join it—to reevaluate their values, theology, practice, and relationships. Unintentionally, the merger contributed to the development and growth of several "Anabaptist-related" networks made up of congregations that for a variety of reasons chose not to join the new denomination. It is arguable that the merger disrupted the sense of "Christendom" for both General Conference Mennonites and (Old) Mennonite Church Mennonites.

The two merged denominations were left with fewer members and congregations than they had begun with. For some, leaving the new denomination had been a journey of years, even decades, that began well before the merger itself, but that occurred as their perception of the disruption became more intense.

For some of those who stayed, the merger also felt disrupting, the natural result of the coming together of two denominations that had grown up relating to one another but with separate identities, values, cultures, and organizational structures. General Conference members were more congregational, with decisions being made at the level of the congregation. (Old) Mennonite Church members were accustomed to greater organizational hierarchy, with decisions being made by denominational and area conference leadership. Bringing together these two traditions may have been symbolic for some of the disruption taking place in their own sphere of Christendom and of crisis in the church.

Comments by respondents who remain in the post-transformation denomination reflect these concerns:

- I have waning enthusiasm for the church in general since the formation of MC USA; many good congregations have left us, so we are burdened with financial needs.
- I believe that the recent energy and expenses in merging the churches to USA was a complete waste. There was no gain, but forced many congregations to make a decision and they left. So, who are we now—perhaps the Elitists?
- Polity is still a very real issue in the integration of the MC/GC churches. This has impacted leadership to outreach. Are we really accomplishing more? Are we really more efficient? Now we focus more on this than outreach and the growth of Christ's church.
- Big government doesn't work, so why big churches (Mennonite USA)? The church is people, not buildings and not organization.
- We are more organized year after year, as if organization is going to bring in the kingdom.
- I have appreciated over the years what the Mennonite church has stood for—its biblical values and teachings, but am saddened to see the falling away and fitting into the culture around it. I'm concerned about what MC USA is going to bring forth.

The denomination continues to struggle with governance and polity issues, and while these are important, they are largely structural symptoms of deeper cultural and spiritual tensions felt by members and leaders in the wake of the merger. All of this is not to argue against the integration of the two denominations, but rather to suggest that the merger was one of several factors that contributed to Mennonite member perceptions of disruption, change, and crisis in their church.

The findings of Mennonite Member Profile 2006 show that congregations are more important to members than are denominations and area conferences. Among members of Mennonite Church USA, 34% say they are "very strongly" committed to the denomination and 12% to their area conference. In comparison, 58% are "very strongly" committed to their local congregation. While there is some variance across regions of the United States, the patterns of commitment remain the same: congregation is most important, followed by the denomination, and then area conference.

Table 7.1	Regional differences in personal commitment to the church			
Very strong commitment to...	**East**	**Midwest**	**West**	**South**
Congregation	61	54	63	66
Area conference	16	10	9	13
Denomination	32	35	37	36
			Percent	

Noteworthy also is the fact that Mennonites are almost as strongly committed to the broader Christian church as they are to their own denomination. Area conferences barely register in commitment of members relative to other areas of the church, despite the fact that in the new denomination area conferences perform the important roles of credentialing pastors and establishing member guidelines for congregations.

Further analysis shows that commitment to area conference is closely correlated with commitment to the denomination. In other words, those who are highly committed to the denomination are more likely to be highly committed to the area conference; the inverse also is true. In addition, while age is correlated with commitment to both denomination and area conference, it is most strongly related to area conference commitment. That is, older persons are more committed than younger to both the denomination and area conference, but this relationship is even stronger for area conferences. Young people identify less with their area conferences than the denomination.

A crisis of individualism. In 1985, Robert Bellah and four colleagues wrote a book about American religion that has become a sociological classic, largely for their insight about the increased individualism of Americans. Religion, for Americans, has become a private and individual part of their lives. One respondent that they interviewed, for example, had created her own religion, which she called "Sheilaism," based on her name, Sheila.[9] This rise in individualism among Christians has threatened our ability and willingness to share the gospel with neighbors and friends, since religion has become like money and sex—a private matter. A simultaneous outcome has been the weakening of Christian faith among some members, who in a pluralistic world believe that all religions and faith traditions are relatively equivalent. For some, Jesus has become just one of many ways to salvation.

In attempting to tap the extent of individualism among Mennonites, we asked several questions that yielded the following findings:

- 30% agree that "church denominations do not matter to me; one is as good as another."
- 38% agree that "the organized church does not really matter; personal faith is what counts."
- 18% agree that "the church has no business being involved in my personal lifestyle decisions."
- 49% agree that "too much emphasis on Mennonite beliefs gets in the way of the true message of the gospel."
- 56% agree that faith is a "private matter between me and God."
- 37% agree that "Muslims and Christians worship the same God." At the same time, 75% believe that "Christians should do all they can to convert Muslims to Christ."

Crisis in identity. Respondents were given eleven religious descriptors and first asked to mark the two that best described their beliefs. Two-thirds of members identified themselves as Mennonite, Anabaptist, or both. Among the one-third who did not, 34% called themselves spiritual, 26% evangelical, 5% charismatic, and 2%

Table 7.2	Religious identities of members		
	2006	Racial/Ethnic	Pastor
Fundamentalist	6	6	2
Anabaptist	45	19	72
Evangelical	18	30	30
Mennonite	48	31	42
Charismatic/Pentecostal	4	16	7
Spiritual	31	33	21
Mainline	3	3	0
	Percent		

Pentecostal. Eighty-four percent of pastors chose Anabaptist or Mennonite, as did 40% of Racial/Ethnic members and 52% of those who have been members in other denominations.

Members as a whole were equally likely to call themselves Anabaptist or Mennonite, followed by spiritual and then evangelical. There was little identification among members as fundamentalists, charismatics/Pentecostals, or mainline Protestants. Racial/Ethnic members were more likely to call themselves Mennonite than Anabaptist—in fact, fewer than 20% identify as Anabaptist. And Racial/Ethnic members were just as likely to call themselves spiritual as they were to identify as Mennonite. They were no more likely than other members to identify as fundamentalists, but four times more likely to call themselves charismatic or Pentecostal. Pastors, on the other hand, are much more likely to identify as Anabaptists— nearly three-quarters—than as Mennonites. They are as likely to call themselves evangelical as are Racial/Ethnic members. And while pastors are similar to Racial/Ethnic members in their understanding of and experience with the Holy Spirit, they do not readily identify as charismatic or Pentecostal.

Greeley and Hout report that six percent of all Americans are charismatic or associated with the charismatic movement. Among conservative Protestants in the United States, 8% are charismatic or associated with the charismatic movement and among mainline Protestants only 5%. Among African-Americans in the study that they cite, 12% are charismatic.[10]

Members expressed ambivalence about their religious identity. Forty-nine percent agreed that too much emphasis on Mennonite beliefs gets in the way of the true message of the gospel. Members were also asked whether they agreed or disagreed that "Mennonite teachings more accurately reflect the Word of God than the teachings of other denominations." In 1972, 30% of members completely agreed with this statement. By 2006, however, only 8% did so. Interestingly, however, both Racial/Ethnic members and pastors in 2006 were more likely than other Mennonites to agree that Mennonite teachings more accurately reflect the Word of God.

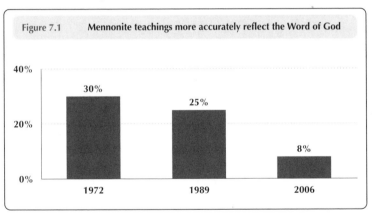

Figure 7.1   Mennonite teachings more accurately reflect the Word of God

Racial/Ethnic challenges and opportunities. Unfortunately, the growth of Racial/Ethnic Mennonite congregations is little known or recognized by most whites within the denomination. But Mennonites do reflect honestly their lack of awareness. When asked whether Racial/Ethnic members have more or fewer opportunities than other Mennonites, 41% reported they were "unsure."

When asked how important it was that Mennonite Church USA leaders reflect racial and ethnic diversity of the denomination, whites and Racial/Ethnic members responded differently. While 49% of Racial/Ethnic members believe that leadership diversity is very important, only 26% of whites believe so. When asked whether they support intentional efforts to hire and promote Racial/Ethnic minorities to overcome patterns of racism in our society, 25% of Racial/Ethnic members strongly support such efforts, compared to 4% of whites. Finally, when asked how important it is that church leaders discuss and address issues of race and racism, 44% of Racial/Ethnic members said that it is very important, compared to 27% of whites.

These findings reinforce the fact that many Mennonites are unaware of the realities of Racial/Ethnic members in their own church. The alienation that these members and congregations feel from the larger church was apparent as I visited pastors in Philadelphia, Chicago, and Los Angeles. Some shared stories of specific instances in which the larger church had failed to include them in decision making and in partnership.

These pastors and congregations have good reason to feel as they do. For most white Americans, race is not an important category for understanding the world. Race and ethnic identity for Anglos has little negative impact on their everyday lives. For whites, race is a "taken for granted" social category that most think little about. For those who are Racial/Ethnic, however, the category of race continues to be a relevant and determining factor in many areas, including life expectancy, occupational and educational opportunities, choice of housing, income, and more.

A regional challenge. As part of a small denomination of just 109,000 members, Mennonite Church USA is spread from coast to coast and from the Canadian border to the Mexico. The distribution of members and the regional differences among them present challenges to unity and decision making at the denominational level. The decision in 2006 by Lancaster Mennonite Conference not to ordain women is one example of the challenge, but the denomination faces similar tensions on other issues.

Those in the East (52%) and South (64%) are least likely to support the ordination of women, and those in the Midwest (75%) and West (82%) most likely. Attitudes about homosexuality differ with western (41%) and midwestern (38%) Mennonites more willing to accept practicing homosexuals as members than southern (26%) and eastern Mennonites (21%).

Several other examples of important regional differences in belief and practice include:

- Western Mennonites are baptized later than Mennonites in other regions—on average at 15.2 years of age, compared to 13.7 to 14.0 years of age in other area conferences.
- Weekly church attendance is lowest in the Midwest and West (77%) and highest in the East (86%). Sunday school attendance also differs by region, with 42% attending in the West and 61% attending in the East.
- Eastern Mennonites are most evangelical in their identity, with 89% identifying as being born again, compared to 71% in the Midwest, 72% in the West, and 83% in the South.
- Those in the Midwest are least likely to read the Bible daily (28%) with those in the East most likely (37%). Midwesterners are also least likely to embrace a literal view of Scripture, while those in the East are most likely to do so.

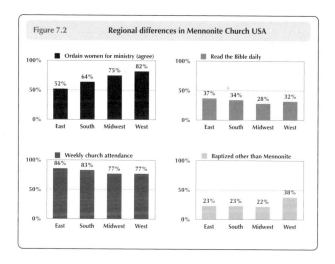

Figure 7.2   Regional differences in Mennonite Church USA

Only a few variables revealed little regional difference—average age of members, the likelihood of members to identify as Anabaptist, personal commitment to the denomination, and the importance of distinctive Mennonite beliefs. Answers to these items did not vary significantly by region.

Conclusion

Walter Brueggemann describes the fall of Jerusalem as the dismantling of "meaning and power." In their crisis of "life and faith," the people of God had to "let go of the old world of king and temple that God had now taken" and "receive from God's hand a new world which it did not believe possible and which was not the one it would have preferred or chosen."[11]

This is similar to the crisis in which Mennonites today find themselves, having to "let go" of old denominational structures and relationships and to "receive . . . a new world" that some would not have "preferred or chosen." At the same time, members keenly feel the loss of their former Mennonite "Christendom" with its familiarity and predictability. New denominational structures and agencies, the growth of members who are not Mennonite, increased assimilation into the broader culture, the growth of Racial/Ethnic congregations and the challenge of racism, a decline in an Anabaptist identity, the aging of members, and the emergence of numerous Anabaptist related networks of congregations, all represent ways members are being forced to accept their liminality.

While these changes have disrupted the church and its members, from a missional perspective we can affirm that God's Spirit has sent them to Mennonite Church USA for our renewal and transformation. The "meaning and power" of those in the middle of the church is being questioned and challenged by those on the margins. The longer we resist these realities, the greater the likelihood that the church as we know it will disappear into oblivion. The vector today is not moving in a positive direction for white, middle-class, Mennonite congregations that are stuck in the middle. Unless we address this reality, we will miss the new move of God's Spirit among us. If we embrace this moment, we have a rare opportunity for renewal and to truly live into our missional calling. If we fail to do so, I am afraid we will go the way of other North American denominations—continued aging of members, ongoing loss of our young people, and further shuttering of our churches.

This predicament should be enough to cause us to consider a missional future. In fact, Mennonites and Anabaptists should find something old-fashioned and familiar about missional language and theology. Such language returns us to discussions about our place in the larger culture and our calling as God's people to be a witness to that culture. These kinds of questions are rooted deeply in our past and provide a pathway for us to engage in a renewed way the richness of a history and theology developed by early Anabaptists. They also lived in the midst of widespread change and disruption, out of which God's Spirit breathed new life and birthed new signs of the kingdom.

8

Exiled in Babylon

This is what the LORD Almighty, the God of Israel, says to all
those I carried into exile from Jerusalem to Babylon: "Build
houses and settle down; plant gardens and eat what they pro-
duce. Marry and have sons and daughters; find wives for your
sons and give your daughters in marriage, so that they too may
have sons and daughters. Increase in number there; do not
decrease. Also, seek the peace and prosperity of the city to
which I have carried you into exile. Pray to the LORD for it,
because if it prospers, you too will prosper." . . .

"For I know the plans I have for you," declares the LORD,
"plans to prosper you and not to harm you, plans to give you
hope and a future. Then you will call upon me and come and
pray to me, and I will listen to you. You will seek me and find
me when you seek me with all your heart. I will be found by
you," declares the LORD, "and will bring you back from captivity. I will gather you from all the nations and places where I have
banished you," declares the LORD, "and will bring you back to
the place from which I carried you into exile."

—Jeremiah 29:4-7, 11-14

Exile in Babylon was a serious blow to God's people. Filled with
grief at the loss of their homeland and anxiety about living among
pagans, they penned their sorrows in Psalm 137:

By the rivers of Babylon we sat and wept when we remem-
bered Zion. There on the poplars we hung our harps, for
there our captors asked us for songs, our tormentors
demanded songs of joy; they said, "Sing us one of the songs
of Zion!" How can we sing the songs of the LORD while in
a foreign land? (vv. 1-4)

Always the oddball, Jeremiah responded to their grief in a way
that probably felt as cruel as his earlier prophecies of Jerusalem's

destruction. Again his words were contrary to what other prophets were telling the exiles. In essence, Jeremiah said to them, "Get over it! Sing your songs anyway! God has ordained your predicament, and if you just cooperate with God's plans, you will prosper! In fact, pray for Babylonia. Pray that the shalom of God's kingdom will come to it, because 'if it prospers, you too will prosper.'"

Then Jeremiah recorded some of the best-known verses of the Bible, often read by Christians today in the midst of difficulty: "'For I know the plans I have for you,' declares the LORD, 'plans to prosper you and not to harm you, plans to give you hope and a future.'" God had not forgotten his people, nor *would* God forget them. Jeremiah repeatedly assured the people that cooperation with God's "anointed" King Nebuchadnezzar would bring safety and security. The only requirement was that they obey Yahweh, something they had not done so well in Judah. Could they do any better in a foreign land?

Exiled or Colonized?

Through Jeremiah, God instructed the new exiles to "pursue the peace and prosperity of the city" where they were now in residence. They were to settle down and prosper. At the same time they were not to become so comfortable that they would forget their homeland. God promised they would return to Judah: "I will gather you from all the nations and places where I have banished you . . . back to the place from which I carried you into exile." In other words, they were to be ambassadors but not citizens of Babylon. However, when King Cyrus of Persia allowed the exiles to return to Judah in 539 BC, many chose not to do so. They had become too invested in a land they were to visit but not call home; they had become fully assimilated and had forgotten who they were and where they came from.

Missional theologian Alan Roxburgh uses the metaphor of "colonization" to describe this kind of assimilation, something he argues has happened to the North American church today. He says, "[The] values, habits and frameworks of the wider culture" have effectively colonized "the churches and denominations of North America."[1] Pushing this metaphor further, we might say that the broader culture and society have taken over the church just as parasites take over their host, feeding off it and destroying it. Like many of the Jews in Babylon, American Christians, including some Mennonites have been co-opted and are now no different from the broader culture. With a few exceptions, it is arguable that the church in North America sits firmly in the middle of that culture. No longer speaking from the margins, it has all but lost a prophetic voice to challenge sin, including injustice, oppression, and violence.

Borrowing the language of "Babylonian captivity" to describe modern evangelicalism, Ron Sider argues that the Christianity of Americans is being destroyed by "scandalous behavior."

> By their daily activity, most 'Christians' regularly commit treason. With their mouths they claim that Jesus is Lord, but with their actions they demonstrate allegiance to money, sex, and self-fulfillment. . . . American popular culture is sick, sick unto death. And the illness has swept through the church. Hollywood's outrageous sexual values and crazy consumerism are rooted in pervasive, long-standing individualism and materialism that have taken deep root in our culture. . . . The gospel of self-fulfillment now reigns.[2]

Principles for Exiles

But of course, this was never God's plan for God's people. In fact, there were some exiles who did live faithfully in Babylon and from whom we can learn key principles about faithful exile living. Daniel, his three friends Shadrach, Meshach, and Abednego, as well as Ezra, Nehemiah, and Esther each teach us something about how to be exiles who are "in the world but not of the world." What are some of these principles?

They never forget their identity. Exiles do not forget who they are or where they came from—their identity is clear. Daniel and his three friends "resolved not to defile" themselves by eating and drinking the royal food and wine of Babylon (Daniel 1:8). Making an agreement with their guard to eat only vegetables, they became stronger and healthier than those who ate the royal food. Though selected to be among the elite in Babylon, they would not compromise God's dietary restrictions. Queen Esther is another example of one who did not forget who she was, taking important risks for the sake of God's people. Knowing that the king could kill her for approaching his throne without permission, she did so anyway because of her identity as one of God's people, thus preventing their annihilation.

Living out its identity as clearly as these exiles will mean that from time to time the church will appear a bit offbeat (perhaps a lot offbeat!), contrasting with the surrounding culture and society. This requirement for the church is deeply rooted in the teachings of Jesus: "[The] call to be a countercultural community runs all through the New Testament. Jesus warned that the world would hate his followers because they refused to live like the world. The New Testament writers used the images of aliens and strangers to describe the church."[3]

They are always loyal to Yahweh. While willing to work on behalf of Babylon and submitting to those who had authority over them—even to the point of being called "sons" and "servants of the Babylonians"—faithful exiles stubbornly resisted any compromise of their commitment to Yahweh. This commitment is seen in the refusal of Shadrach, Meshach, and Abednego to bow down to Nebuchadnezzar's ninety-foot-tall image of gold. Their response to Nebuchadnezzar's threats to kill them was uncompromising:

> "O Nebuchadnezzar, we do not need to defend ourselves before you in this matter. If we are thrown into the blazing furnace, the God we serve is able to save us from it, and he will rescue us from your hand, O king. But even if he does not, we want you to know, O king, that we will not serve your gods or worship the image of gold you have set up." (Daniel 3:16-18)

The commitment of these young men to serve their Babylonian masters was second to their commitment to serve Yahweh first and foremost.

They never defend themselves. Exiles do not defend themselves when threatened. They simply acknowledge their allegiance to God and willingly accept the consequences of that allegiance, even if this means death. This was true for the three young men in the fiery furnace, as well as for Daniel, who went to the lion's den because of his insistence on praying daily to Yahweh.

They understand God's plans and purposes. Exiles understand keenly that they are part of God's plans and purposes. They recognize that their achievements and experiences in exile, whether easy or difficult, are ordained by a sovereign God. Mordecai, when discussing his plan for the deliverance of God's people with his niece Esther, motivated her by saying:

> "Do not think that because you are in the king's house you alone of all the Jews will escape. For if you remain silent at this time, relief and deliverance for the Jews will arise from another place, but you and your father's family will perish. And who knows but that you have come to royal position for such a time as this." (Esther 4:13-14)

And Joseph, an exile from an earlier period in the Old Testament, readily forgave his brothers who had sent him into Egypt, understanding the big picture of God's plans and purposes. "Don't be afraid," Joseph said to them. "Am I in the place of God? You intended to harm me, but God intended it for good to accomplish what is now being done, the saving of many lives" (Genesis 50:19-20).

Mennonites in Exile

While there are likely others, these four principles provide a framework for thinking about our own exile and give some direction for avoiding colonization. These principles are also evident in the writings and experiences of early Anabaptists in Europe, many of whom faced death for their uncompromising commitment to Jesus Christ. Martyrdom created a sense of exile for these Anabaptists, whose world was divided into "two spheres" composed of the "law of the sword," or the government, and the "perfection of Christ," or the kingdom of God.[4] In fact, for Mennonites, more than many other Christian traditions, exile may be the dominant metaphor for reflecting upon our history.

In this chapter we will consider the lives and lifestyles of Mennonites today, holding up these principles of exile as a backdrop for reflection on a number of questions, including, Do Mennonites still live with any sense of being in exile? To what extent have Mennonites been colonized by the broader American culture? Are Mennonites seeking the peace and prosperity of the world to which they have been called? Have Mennonites retained a sense of identity as God's people? Do Mennonites recognize God's plans and purposes? While this chapter will not directly answer all of these questions with data from Mennonite Member Profile 2006, it will provide some insight for ongoing discussion of these questions.

Two kingdoms. John Roth describes the foundation of a Mennonite view of two kingdoms this way:

> The concept of the two kingdoms begins with the recognition that all of creation is engaged in a cosmic battle, a spiritual warfare between good and evil. Since the story of the fall in Genesis 3, salvation history . . . is a dramatic account of the persistent struggle between faithfulness to God's intentions for the world and the stubborn reality of human selfishness, greed, and violence. This struggle gives meaning to the language of sin, salvation, and redemption. It reminds us that something of utmost importance is at stake. Even though Christians know that the ultimate outcome of this battle has already been decided . . . we nonetheless find ourselves faced with a genuine choice.[5]

This choice—to serve the purposes of God's kingdom or the purposes of the world—are ever before the exile, just as they were before Daniel and his three friends.

Several questions in Mennonite Member Profile 2006 addressed member beliefs about their awareness of the kingdom of God and the kingdom of the world and any conflict they feel between these two kingdoms. Sixty-four percent of Mennonites completely agreed that there is a "clear difference between the 'kingdom of God' and the 'kingdom of this world.'" When asked about Christian involvement in the kingdom of this world, only

22% completely agreed that Christians should "avoid" such involvements. While Mennonite members see a distinction between the kingdom of God and the kingdom of the world, relatively few believe that involvement in the world's kingdom should be avoided.

Racial/Ethnic members (80%) and pastors (75%) were both more likely than others to completely agree about the difference between the kingdom of God and the kingdom of the world. Pastors (12%) were less likely than members to believe that involvements in the world should be avoided, but Racial/Ethnic members were more favorable toward such avoidance (41%).

The tendency for pastors to discourage avoidance of the world was also reflected in another question, which asked how "Christians should relate to popular culture." In this question, 48% of pastors would choose to engage the culture "and try to make it better," compared to 33% of members and 38% of Racial/Ethnic members. Relative to members, pastors appear to believe that part of the Christian calling is to be engaged in the broader culture.

Members were also asked how much conflict they experience between "Mennonite beliefs and practices and the beliefs and practices of the larger society." Seventy-three percent of members said that they experience some level of conflict compared to 92% of pastors and only 49% of Racial/Ethnic members. These findings may reflect the differences among members, pastors, and Racial/Ethnic members in their willingness to engage the broader culture. Pastors, who most believe the culture should be engaged, also feel the most tension. Racial/Ethnic members, who are least likely to want to engage the culture, feel the least tension.

As a whole, members today (73%) feel more conflict than in 1989 (57%), which may be related to the increased assimilation of members into the broader culture. While members are more assimilated today, they appear to also feel more conflict between the two kingdoms within which they operate.

Separation of church and state. The separation of church and state was an important ingredient for early Anabaptists, who were perhaps the first to insist on the separation of these two powers.

Living at a time when the "church and state were inextricably fused," these believers in Jesus wanted to ensure that the "Christian's allegiance to the church comes before the demands of obedience to the state."[6] For Anabaptists, loyalty to Christ could not be compromised by loyalty to any other power.

While many Americans assume the separation of church and state in the United States, actual practice often blurs the lines between the two, including among Mennonites members, as the following findings reveal. Forty-eighty percent of Mennonites believe that "America is a Christian nation," compared to only 8% of pastors. Sixty-seven percent of Mennonites agree that it is "all right for Mennonites to pledge allegiance to the flag" (31% of pastors), and 35% of members are comfortable with an American flag inside a Mennonite church—but only 9% of pastors.

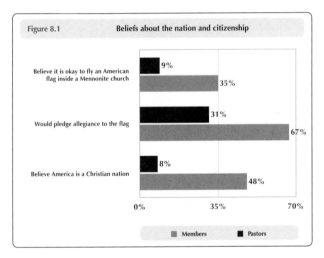

Figure 8.1   Beliefs about the nation and citizenship

These findings show important differences among members and the pastors who lead them. Pastors are more likely to recognize two kingdoms and more likely to believe that Christians should engage the kingdom of the world. But pastors are least likely to embrace the nation-state. Involvement in the kingdom of the world, for pastors, is not about being co-opted by their country.

Government and political action. Mennonites believe that the church is God's new nation as described in 1 Peter 2:9: "a chosen people, a royal priesthood, a holy nation, a people belonging to God." These are the same words used to describe God's people in the Old Testament. Says Helmut Harder, Mennonite theologian and writer of a study guide to accompany *The Confession of Faith from a Mennonite Perspective*:

> While the people of Israel were a nation of one bloodline, the church is a "nation" comprised of people from many nations. While the Old Testament people were bent on claiming nationhood within their own geographical boundary, the church is a "nation" that knows no boundaries. While the Old Testament people desired their earthly king, the church recognizes Christ, the heavenly king, as their supreme head.[7]

Living with this understanding has meant that Mennonites have historically prayed for and respected those in governing authority, but have been hesitant to become overly committed to government service or to look at political engagement as a way to bring about societal reform.

Evidence from Mennonite Member Profile 2006, however, shows substantial change in the relationship of Mennonites to government and politics. In addition, Racial/Ethnic members are more likely than other Mennonites to support political action, despite the finding I noted earlier in which they were more likely than other Mennonites to avoid engagement with the world. The support for political involvement among Racial/Ethnic members is likely due to the fact that for racial and ethnic minorities in the United States, political activism and government intervention have been critical in addressing racism and creating greater equality.

- Thirty-four percent of Racial/Ethnic members completely agree that "Christians should actively participate in politics to help improve society," compared to 11% of pastors and 18% of members.
- Forty-two percent of Racial/Ethnic members completely agree that "church leaders should try to influence government leaders on issues like war, peace, racism, and poverty," compared to 26% of pastors and 27% of members.

- When asked how Christians should relate to government, 27% of Racial/Ethnic members responded with "actively participate in government to improve it," compared to 13% of pastors and 21% of members.

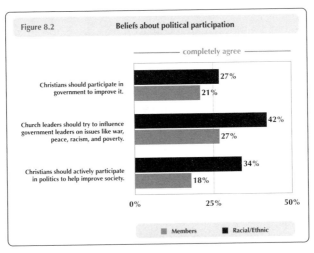

Figure 8.2   **Beliefs about political participation**

——— completely agree ———

Christians should participate in government to improve it.
27%
21%

Church leaders should try to influence government leaders on issues like war, peace, racism, and poverty.
42%
27%

Christians should actively participate in politics to help improve society.
34%
18%

0%   25%   50%

■ Members   ■ Racial/Ethnic

The support of Racial/Ethnic members for engaging the government may also partially explain why Racial/Ethnic members are more willing than other Mennonites to swear oaths and to file lawsuits—both historic Anabaptist prohibitions. Fifty-nine percent of Racial/Ethnic members agree that it is all right for a Christian to file a lawsuit, compared to 43% of other members and only 19% of pastors. Fifty-nine percent of Racial/Ethnic members also agree that it is all right to swear an oath in court, while 46% of other members say the same and 28% of pastors. On the other hand, Racial/Ethnic members may be reflecting the relative newness of some of them to Anabaptist teachings, and the fact that their theology and practice continues to be shaped. It is hardly fair to charge Racial/Ethnic members with being less Anabaptist when many of them are first generation Mennonites.

Peacemaking and the military. Roth describes historic Mennonite commitments to peacemaking and nonviolence.

> At the heart of the Mennonite understanding of Christian discipleship and the new creation are Christ's teachings in the gospels regarding love and service. . . . Perhaps no point is more foundational to this new orientation than Christ's admonition to love our enemies. . . . It would seem much more logical, of course, to argue that we should defend our interests, punish those who threaten us, draw a line between good and evil, and give evildoers what they have coming to them. . . . Christ teaches his disciples to love even those who persecute them, or mistreat them, or are their enemies.[8]

Even though exiles face insecurity and danger, they are called to lay down their lives for their Lord rather than to defend themselves. The posture of the exile in the face of threats is a nonresistant one, and this was the historic teaching of Anabaptists.

As noted earlier, Mennonite support for nonresistance has declined over thirty-five years. Among members today, 21% would choose regular or noncombatant military service and 10% of members who were unsure what they would do. Racial/Ethnic members are more likely to choose military service with 33% saying they would do so but 26% saying they were not sure.

Racial/Ethnic members were also slightly more likely to have served in the military, with 6% having such experience, compared to 4% of other members and 4% of pastors. Racial/Ethnic members were also slightly more likely to have family members who served in the military—39% compared to 33% of other members and 23% of pastors.

When evaluating the U.S. war in Iraq, 24% of Mennonites agree that the United States did "the right thing" in going to war against Iraq—8% of pastors agree and 26% of Racial/Ethnic members.

Racial/Ethnic members were more likely to agree (69% compared to 56% of other members) that "it is all right for Christians to be in noncombatant service in the armed forces" and less likely to agree that "it is wrong for Christians to fight in any war" (55% of Racial/Ethnic members compared to 65% of other members). However, Racial/Ethnic members (88%) are as likely as other members (85%) to agree that "complete nonviolence as a way of living is very important to me" and that "peacemaking is a central theme of the gospel" (93% for both).

These findings suggest that Racial/Ethnic members are just as likely as other Mennonites to embrace a theology of peacemaking, but their commitment to political action, as well as the relative newness of some of them to Anabaptist theology, may make them more willing to be involved in military service.

Nonconformity to the world. Until the mid to late twentieth century, many Mennonites embraced nonconformity to the world as a sign of faithfulness to Jesus Christ. This understanding of faithfulness was based on Paul's commandment in Romans 12:2: "Do not conform any longer to the pattern of this world, but be transformed by the renewing of your mind." For many Mennonites, this meant restrictions on dress, a commitment by women to wear the prayer covering, limits on the kinds of recreational activities one engaged in, and more. Nonconformity also contributed to a simpler lifestyle, another value of earlier Mennonites. But as I have indicated previously, Mennonites have become more like the broader society with higher levels of education, more professional occupations, and less rural residence. Members were asked whether "living a simple lifestyle is an important part of my Christian witness." Forty-six percent of Racial/Ethnic members completely agreed that it is compared to 33% of other members.

Members were asked their opinions about twenty-six behaviors. Other than around issues of sexuality, Mennonites show little consensus about what they consider morally wrong. They have also changed their views substantially in defining what is wrong and what is not.

Mennonites are most likely to agree about the wrongness of sexual behaviors, although there is some variation as well as change since 1972. In 2006, extramarital sex was considered "always wrong" by 94% of members, followed by homosexual relations (79%) and premarital sex (74%). Other sexually related behaviors also received strong affirmation by members as always wrong, including watching X-rated movies (77%) and viewing pornography (81%).

Table 8.1   Members who consider the following activities "always wrong"

Activity	Percent	Activity	Percent
Extramarital sexual intercourse	94	Owning stock in companies that make war goods	30
Viewing pornographic materials	81	Drinking alcohol	26
Homosexual relations between consenting adults	79	Copying a music CD for a friend	25
Watching X-rated (adult) movies	77	Marriage between a Christian and a non-Christian	24
Premarital sexual intercourse	74	Entering the armed forces	23
Smoking marijuana	71	Buying an expensive sports car	14
Smoking cigarettes	65	Remarriage while the former spouse is living	14
Using profanity (cursing)	63	Divorce	9
Playing violent computer or video games	57	Spanking children	7
Gambling	50	Dancing	7
Wearing immodest clothing	45	Buying stylish and fashionable clothing	6
Buying government lottery tickets	38	Working as a police officer	5

With the exception of alcohol, substance use and abuse are the second category of behaviors that Mennonites most agree on. Seventy percent believe that smoking marijuana is always wrong and 65% that smoking cigarettes is always wrong. Only 26% of members, however, believe that alcohol use is always wrong.

Behaviors next considered "always wrong" were using profanity (63%), abortion (57%), playing violent video/computer games (51%), and gambling (50%).

The order of the remaining behaviors was wearing immodest clothing (45%), buying government lottery tickets (38%), owning stock in companies that make war goods (30%), copying a music CD for a friend (25%), marriage between a Christian and non-Christian (24%), entering the armed forces (23%), remarriage while the former spouse is living (14%), buying an expensive sports car (14%), divorce (9%), dancing (7%), spanking children (7%), buying stylish and fashionable clothing (6%), and working as a police officer (5%).

Pastors were different from members in a number of areas, more willing than members to say that the following were always wrong: marriage between a Christian and non-Christian, serving in the armed forces, gambling and the lottery, and immodesty. They were less likely than members to say that substance use, profanity, and abortion were always wrong, among several other behaviors.

There have been changes in the "wrongness" of many of these behaviors by members since 1972. The only behavior that saw no change across time was smoking tobacco. Among behaviors that have seen the most change are the following:

- *Divorce and remarriage.* In 1972 31% of respondents said that divorce was always wrong (including cases of adultery) compared to 9% today who say divorce is always wrong. Sixty percent in 1972 replied that remarriage while a former spouse is living was always wrong, compared to 14% in 2006.
- *Alcohol.* In 1972, 51% said that drinking alcohol even moderately was always wrong, compared to almost half of that percent today (26%).
- *Premarital sex.* In 1972 84% of Mennonites said that premarital sex was always wrong. Attitudes about premarital sex have changed dramatically, even more so than about homosexuality, with only 74% today saying that premarital sex is always wrong.
- *Extramarital sex.* Opposition to adultry has grown since 1972, when 86% of members said extramarital sex was always wrong compared to 94% today.
- *Homosexual relations.* In 1972, 85% of Mennonites said that homosexual relations between consenting adults was always wrong. Fewer believe so today, down six points to 79%. While the vast majority of Mennonites believe that homosexual practice is wrong, more are willing today (31%) to accept practicing homosexuals as members in their churches than in 1989 (22%).
- *Other behaviors.* A number of behaviors that Mennonites long considered vices but about which many have changed their minds today include gambling (from 76% in 1972 to 50% today), and dancing (from 43% in 1972 to 7% today). In these behaviors that would have been considered "worldly" by earlier generations, Mennonites are moving rapidly toward losing their distinctiveness.

These findings suggest major changes in what Mennonites define as right and wrong. In general, the changes support the argument that Mennonites are becoming more conforming to the values

Table 8.2   Changes over three decades in the "wrongness" of behaviors

Always wrong	1972	2006
Divorce	31	9
Remarriage while former spouse living	60	14
Drinking alcohol	51	26
Marriage between different races	18	5
Smoking marijuana	87	70
Smoking tobacco	62	65
Premarital sex	84	74
Extramarital sex	89	94
Homosexual relations	85	79
Owning war stock	39	30
Gambling	76	50
Dancing	43	7
	Percent	

and attitudes of the larger society—looking more like their neighbors and co-workers than was true for Mennonites thirty-five years ago. But again, this should not come as a surprise given the upward mobility of Mennonites, the lessening importance of the church, and the greater exposure to the media.

In some ways, Mennonites are no different from other U.S. Protestants. Ron Sider notes, for example, that 26% of evangelicals do not believe that premarital sex is wrong and that 13% do not believe that extramarital sex is wrong. At the same time, Greeley and Hout found that, like Mennonites, conservative Protestants and mainline Protestants over the past thirty years have both increased their objection to extramarital sex, with 87% (average across thirty years) of conservative Protestants and 75% of mainline Protestants opposed.[9]

Mennonites are similar to other conservative Protestants in their opposition to homosexuality, with 85% of conservative Protestants saying it is always wrong (a thirty-year average) compared to 84% of Mennonites during nearly the same period (average across the three member profiles). The thirty-year average for mainline Protestants is only 69%. But opposition to homosexual relations has shown decline among Mennonites as well as conservative Protestants over time. Since 1990 both conservative and mainline Protestants have decreased in their opposition to homosexual relations—a 9% decline among conservative Protestants and a 12% decline among mainline Protestants.[10] Among Mennonites, the percentage saying that homosexual relations are always wrong has declined by 10% since 1989.

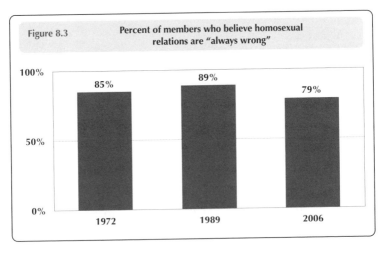

Figure 8.3   **Percent of members who believe homosexual relations are "always wrong"**

Rates of viewing X-rated movies are higher among both conservative Protestants and mainline Protestants than among Mennonites. Nine percent of Mennonites have viewed an X-rated film over the past year, compared with 18% of conservative Protestants and 19% of mainline Protestants.[11]

In general, Mennonite attitudes about certain behaviors have changed dramatically across thirty years. Their attitudes in general mirror those of other U.S. Christians, with less opposition to homosexuality than two decades ago but greater opposition to extramarital sexual relations. While Mennonites have changed, these changes have paralleled those of other North American denominations.

Marriage and family. In one study of Americans, the percentage of born-again Christians who have experienced divorce (33%) is about the same as non-born again Americans (34%). And for

90% of those who are born again and divorced, the divorce came after their conversion to Christ. Another study found conservative Protestants are even more likely to divorce than others.[12]

Among Mennonites, only 2% are currently divorced and only 10% have ever experienced divorce. The percentage currently divorced has remained largely unchanged for thirty-five years. Mennonites differ substantially from the broader society in the stability of their marriages and families.

Twenty-five percent of all born-again persons have lived with someone of the opposite sex before marriage, compared to 33% of Americans as a whole. Only 10% of Mennonite members have ever lived with someone in a romantic relationship without being married to that person.

One of the interesting findings of Greeley and Hout is the strong opposition of conservative Protestants to homosexuality but declining opposition to premarital sex. Say Greeley and Hout, "The majority of both groups [conservative Protestant and mainline Protestant] . . . freely engage in premarital sex. One hears little protest from the clergy at the annual meetings of the conservative denominations."[13] While teaching against homosexuality, admonishment about premarital sex has declined among Protestants. The rates of change among Mennonites suggest a similar pattern.

Conclusion

We began this chapter asking several questions: Do Mennonites still live with any sense of being in exile? To what extent have Mennonites been colonized by the broader American culture? Are Mennonites seeking the peace and prosperity of the world to which they have been called? Have Mennonites retained a sense of identity as God's people? Do Mennonites recognize God's plans and purposes?

Mennonites came to America with a deep sense of exile nurtured by persecution in Europe. Once in America however, Mennonites tended to cloister themselves away from the pressures and temptations of the world. But over time, Mennonites have become increasingly educated, more professional, and less rural. With those changes came changes in attitudes about moral issues that at one time partly defined Mennonite distinctiveness. The data from this chapter suggest that Mennonites are losing at least some of the distinctives that once defined them.

Apart from Racial/Ethnic Mennonites, half of whom are first-generation immigrants to the United States, it is not clear that most Mennonites live with an ongoing sense of exile. For some of us, I suspect that our history and theology have stayed too long in our heads or that their demands are just too great. As a result, we have accepted something softer, less demanding, more affirming and respectable. As Mennonites who have become assimilated, we have moved from the margins of the surrounding society into its middle.

Mennonites in the 1970s had lower levels of assimilation; there was greater difference between the world and the church by some objective indicators. It is possible that those were not important differences and that we are better off without them. At the same time, they served several functions that the church now misses: they marginalized Mennonites and were important symbols of that marginalization to both society and themselves.

I am not suggesting that Mennonites return to an earlier period of Christendom, where they sequestered themselves from the larger culture by dress and lifestyle distinctives. I do wonder, however, if we shouldn't be doing two things at once: connecting to the broader culture while at the same time spiritually discerning what distinguishes us from that culture. Such a contrast community will face tensions on all sides—from the church, the world, and in between. But such a community will also fulfill its missional calling more fully than one that either avoids the culture or fully embraces it.

9

Journeying Toward God's Reign

"At that time," declares the LORD, "I will be the God of all the clans of Israel, and they will be my people." This is what the LORD says: "The people who survive the sword will find favor in the desert; I will come to give rest to Israel."

The LORD appeared to us in the past, saying: "I have loved you with an everlasting love; I have drawn you with loving-kindness. I will build you up again and you will be rebuilt, O Virgin Israel. Again you will take up your tambourines and go out to dance with the joyful. Again you will plant vineyards on the hills of Samaria; the farmers will plant them and enjoy their fruit. There will be a day when watchmen cry out on the hills of Ephraim, 'Come, let us go up to Zion, to the LORD our God.'"

This is what the LORD says: "Sing with joy for Jacob; shout for the foremost of the nations. Make your praises heard, and say, 'O LORD, save your people, the remnant of Israel.' See, I will bring them from the land of the north and gather them from the ends of the earth. Among them will be the blind and the lame, expectant mothers and women in labor; a great throng will return. They will come with weeping; they will pray as I lead them back. I will lead them beside streams of water on a level path where they will not stumble, because I am Israel's father, and Ephraim is my firstborn son." . . .

This is what the LORD says: "Restrain your voice from weeping and your eyes from tears, for your work will be rewarded," declares the LORD. "They will return from the land of the enemy. So there is hope for your future," declares the LORD. "Your children will return to their own land." . . .

"Set up road signs and put up guideposts. Take note of the highway, the road you take. Return, O Virgin Israel, return to your towns." —Jeremiah 31:1-9, 16-17, 21

Just when all seems lost—whether as a citizen of idolatrous Judah in 587 BC, a member of the lukewarm church of Laodicea in the first century AD, or as a Mennonite follower of Jesus in North America today—suddenly God announces the best news possible!

Even as King Nebuchadnezzar and his army were banging on the walls of Jerusalem, God appeared to Jeremiah saying:

> "I will bring Judah and Israel back from captivity and will rebuild them as they were before. I will cleanse them from all the sin they have committed against me and will forgive all their sins of rebellion against me. Then this city will bring me renown, joy, praise and honor before all nations on earth that hear of all the good things I do for it; and they will be in awe and will tremble at the abundant prosperity and peace I provide for it." (Jeremiah 33:7-9)

And to the lukewarm church of Laodicea in the first century, thinking itself healthy, wealthy, and well dressed but actually "wretched, pitiful, poor, blind, and naked," Jesus appeared with the invitation: "Listen! I am standing at the door, knocking; if you hear my voice and open the door, I will come in to you and eat with you, and you with me" (Revelation 3:20 NRSV). And to God's people of Mennonite Church USA today—living in the midst of disruption and crisis—God still speaks, calling us to reclaim our vocation as the "sent people" of God in our homes, across our streets, and around the world.

In God's economy, good news always follows bad news. In fact, good news sounds even better when preceded by bad. After years of struggling with cancer, my doctor's annual report of "No sign of disease" elicits far greater gratitude to God for my health than ever before. In 587 BC the promise of deliverance was more significant because God's people were on the brink of captivity. To the Laodiceans, Jesus' summons to sit down and eat was more meaningful because it followed his rebuke. And to the church today, the invitation to receive God's kingdom rings more clearly in the midst of disruption, chaos, and crisis than it ever did when things in Christendom appeared stable and predictable.

The Qualities of God's Reign

The good news for God's people in the sixth century BC, for the Laodicean church, and for God's people today has always been the same. Ever since sin entered the world, God has been at work to restore all of creation to a relationship with God and the state of wholeness that only Eden knew. God made a covenant to do so immediately after Adam and Eve shared the fruit, saying to the serpent, "And I will put enmity between you and the woman, and between your offspring and hers; he will crush your head, and you will strike his heel" (Genesis 3:15). In that moment, God initiated a plan to restore and redeem human beings back to relationship with God and to one another. The curse of sin would be undone and all would be made right in creation. The kingdom would be restored.

Throughout the Old Testament, God referred to this state of wholeness, well-being, justice, and restoration as shalom, translated most often into English as "peace." "Peace" as defined by the absence of warfare or the presence of personal tranquility, however, misses the full intentions of God's shalom. In what has become known as the "Book of Comfort," (Jeremiah chapters 30-33), sandwiched between messages of judgment, Jeremiah describes the qualities of shalom that would characterize God's reign:

- freedom from oppression (30:8-9),
- peace and security without fear (30:10),
- restoration of health (30:17),
- joy and singing (30:19),
- fulfillment of the purposes of God's heart (30:24),
- rest (31:2),
- planting and rebuilding (31:4-6),
- forgiveness of sins and intimacy with God (31:18-20),
- children will no longer suffer for the sins of their parents (31:29-32),
- education will be unnecessary because God will be the only teacher and all will know God (31:33-34),
- God's covenant will depend only on God's character as seen in creation (31:1-10, 18-38), and
- God's anger will be revealed against all who oppose shalom and the principles of God's kingdom.

Despite God's judgment on a guilty people and despite the destruction of all that they held sacred, God was planning a new future for them. But what God imagined was not ultimately the reconstruction or renovation of the temple or Jerusalem, or the restoration of the exiles as the exclusive people of God. Instead God envisioned a new people in a new relationship with him, one not bound in time or space—a people composed of every tongue and nation brought together by the redeeming and restoring work of the coming Messiah, Jesus Christ.

In the Old Testament, God was so committed to shalom that he introduced the practice of jubilee in the book of Leviticus. In this practice, every fifty years was to be declared a day of rest—a Sabbath for God's people and for creation. In this year, land was given a rest, slaves were released, debts were erased, and land was returned to its original owners.[1]

Jubilee was a grand idea, for it eliminated the margins and redistributed the middle, working against the temptations of homeland security. Because of jubilee, the value of land and slaves actually depreciated over time rather than increased. As jubilee approached, prices of real estate and labor fell! Jubilee regularly restored God's people to their true identity as children of Yahweh and brothers and sisters of one another.

Unfortunately, it is not clear that God's people ever took jubilee very seriously. The temptation to accumulate and worship things rather than Yahweh was too great. Jeremiah (34:13-17) records God's grief at the failure of the people to carry out jubilee. So, for their failure to practice those things that would have brought them closer to God's vision of shalom, God had Judah sacked and its people carried off to Babylon.

God's Reign in Jesus Christ

God's people in the sixth century undoubtedly assumed that Jeremiah's description of shalom was a word for them and their children as they journeyed back to Judah—that they would experience all of the goodness of God that Jeremiah prophesied. And while a restoration of sorts did occur, it was both limited and short-lived. Within two hundred years of the return of the exiles to Jerusalem, Alexander the Great of Greece stormed into Jerusalem and again destroyed the city. He was followed by Syria and then the Romans.

Jeremiah's prophecies were ultimately about the coming of Jesus Christ, who would bring in God's shalom kingdom. Said Jeremiah about the Messiah:

> "In those days and at that time I will make a righteous Branch sprout from David's line; he will do what is just and right in the land. In those days Judah will be saved and Jerusalem will live in safety. This is the name by which it will be called: The LORD Our Righteousness. (33:15-16)

Jeremiah, like other prophets of the Old Testament, was pointing to a renewal of all goodness that had ever been lost. This renewal would come in the arrival of Christ, the incarnate God. In fact, Jesus' birth, life, and resurrection are filled with images of shalom:

- At Jesus' birth angel songs echoed: "Glory to God in the highest, and on earth *peace* to men on whom his favor rests" (Luke 2:14, emphasis added).
- Jesus began his ministry by reading from Isaiah, proclaiming that he had come to fulfill "the year of the Lord's favor" which his listeners would have understood as the year of jubilee. Then Jesus put himself firmly in the middle of shalom themes reading, "The Spirit of the Lord is me, because he has anointed me to preach good news to the poor. He has sent me to proclaim freedom for the prisoners and recovery of sight for the blind, to release the oppressed, to proclaim the year of the Lord's favor" (Luke 4:18-19).
- Following his resurrection and after defeating the powers of death and hell, Jesus appeared to his disciples saying, "*Peace* be with you! As the Father has sent me, I am sending you" (John 20:21, emphasis added). In other words, shalom had come! Then breathing the Holy Spirit upon his disciples, Jesus sent them into the world.

In fact, two things always seem to be connected to the Holy Spirit's coming: the shalom of the kingdom and the command to be sent into the world. The coming of the Holy Spirit at Pentecost had a transforming "shalom" effect on the early church. Luke records that the early converts practiced a lifestyle that one would expect from persons who understood the shalom nature of gospel, sharing things in common, "selling their possessions and goods," and giving to "anyone as he had need" (Acts 2:45). Living so close in time to the life and teaching of Jesus, these earlier followers—empowered by the Holy Spirit—sought to put into practice the shalom teachings of their Lord while faithfully proclaiming God's salvation.

Road Signs for Mennonites Journeying Toward God's Reign

But what does shalom have to do with Mennonites in North America today? And what does God's reign mean for Mennonites in the 21st century, many situated in the middle of their society and culture?

Historically, Mennonites, perhaps more than other Christian traditions, have attempted to embody shalom in their teaching, daily life, and spiritual communities. Mennonites believe that Jesus Christ came to fulfill all of the promises of shalom in establishing God's reign. When Jesus spoke in the Sermon on the Mount, Mennonites hear practical rules for living in God's shalom kingdom. John Roth notes:

> Over and over in the Gospels, Jesus tries to communicate to his disciples that the kingdom he is introducing operates by different principles than those of the kingdoms of this world. In his kingdom, Jesus tells them, "the first will be last." In his kingdom, those who are meek, merciful, and gentle are the ones who will receive a blessing. In his kingdom, love and compassion are more powerful than the coercive force of violence and the threat of physical pain or death. Indeed, it is only by being a servant, by emptying oneself, that the glory and power of God can be revealed and God's will be truly done "on earth as it is in heaven."[2]

As I have shown throughout this book, many of us as followers of Jesus in North America struggle to live within the reality of shalom as we journey toward the reign of God. Instead, we find ourselves focused on our journey up the ladder of mobility—ensuring our security with greater incomes, higher levels of education, and more.

The purpose of this book has been to point to signs of where Mennonites are today and to suggest new avenues we might wish to consider. As we conclude this book, what have we learned? What signs have we observed? In the following pages I address two types of signs: signs of disruption and signs of the kingdom.

Signs of Disruption

As noted throughout this book Mennonites, like members of other denominations and churches in North America, find themselves in the throes of disruption and crisis. Results of Mennonite Member Profile 2006 reflect certain realities.

- *Denominational merger.* The merging of the General Conference Mennonite Church and the (Old) Mennonite Church added to a sense of disruption for some members and likely a confirmation for them that the "Mennonite Christendom" they knew and loved was changing.
- *Aging.* Mennonite Church USA is rapidly aging, with the retirement of baby boomers, the longer life expectancy of older members, and the lower fertility rates of members of child-bearing age. Without an influx of new members, particularly younger members, questions about the future of the denomination may become the dominant concern.
- *Loss of members.* The number of Mennonites in the denomination has declined by nearly 20,000 since 1990, and the total membership now rests just over 100,000 members. How long a denomination of this size can be sustained is a relevant question, particularly when it has ever fewer young members and the members that it does have show less interest in personal evangelism and outreach than in previous profiles. The percentage of new members to the denomination has remained unchanged since 1989. In addition, only 2% of the denomination's members are new Christians. If Mennonite Church USA is to sustain itself, it will have to attract more persons who are not Mennonite. The challenge in doing so is that new members are typically less loyal to the denomination and identify less as Anabaptists. The alternative, however, is the demise of the denomination.
- *Regional differences.* The regional differences among Mennonites are substantial. There are major challenges in uni-

fying a denomination with such vast regional differences
and in creating uniformity and consistency in denominational policies and practices.

- *Governance and polity.* The governance structure of Mennonite Church USA shows tensions between the denomination
and its area conferences. Area conferences hold the credentials
of ministers and have the authority to establish member guidelines for congregations. Members connect with the denomination through their area conference. However, members show
little awareness of or loyalty to their area conferences.

- *Assimilation.* Mennonites have become more assimilated into
the broader culture—with higher levels of education, more
professional occupations, and fewer members on the farm.
This assimilation has created greater uncertainty around historic Mennonite beliefs and practices, and raises questions
about the extent to which Mennonites are reflecting upon and
discerning the critical theological and moral issues of our day.

- *Race/ethnicity.* Mennonite Church USA includes more Racial/
Ethnic members than ever before. But some of these members
feel alienated and marginalized from the larger church, and
many whites are unaware of their reality or of ongoing racism
in both the church and society.

- *Leadership roles.* Pastors and members differ in their understanding of their respective roles. Pastors believe that they
should be preaching, casting vision, and equipping members
for ministry. Members on the other hand, believe that pastors
should primarily preach and take care of the members.
Unless these differences are negotiated, we will continue to
see frustrated pastors leaving their congregations and frustrated congregations in continual search for the ideal pastor.
Congregations must empower pastors to lead and to equip
the members for ministry. A congregation without ministering members will never become a missional congregation.
And a congregation that is not missional will last only as long
as it produces enough of its own children to fill the pews.

- *Politicization.* Mennonites have become more politically
engaged than in the past. Politics, perhaps more than theology, is the driving force of Mennonite attitudes and values.
John Roth's call for a sabbatical from politics is a prophetic word that challenges an ever increasing tendency to
address social and moral problems with political solutions.

- *Disengagement of young adults.* Mennonite young adults are less active in the church than are older adults. Undoubtedly postponing marriage and childbearing along with other Americans, the reentry of young adults back into the church is likely delayed longer than in the past. As many of these members move to urban areas that do not have Mennonite congregations, it is possible many will never return to the denomination.
- *Identity.* Members are less committed to Anabaptist identity than in the past. Today one-third of Mennonites do not identify themselves as Anabaptists or as Mennonites. And they are much more likely to agree that Mennonite teaching is not that much different from the teaching of other denominations. In addition, fewer Mennonites would choose to be conscientious objectors than in the past, again suggesting erosion of historic commitments to nonresistance.
- *Nonconformity.* Changes over the past three decades among Mennonites have created uncertainty about moral issues and nonconformity. A sign of this confusion is the energy around discussions about homosexuality. While clarifying and strengthening the teaching position of the church on this issue is important, the prolonged focus on it has perhaps led the church to ignore a host of other matters including pre-marital sex, divorce, peacemaking, social justice, and evangelism.

While signs of disruption among Mennonites today are numerous, there are also signs of God's kingdom.

Signs of the Kingdom

- *Racial/Ethnic growth.* The growing presence of Racial/ Ethnic members in Mennonite Church USA is one of the greatest signs of the movement of God's Spirit among Mennonites today. *In United by Faith: The Multiracial Congregation as an Answer to the Problem of Race*, Curtiss Paul DeYoung and colleagues argue that the church has no choice but to become multiracial if it is going to embody the shalom of Jesus Christ:

> Now we must move forward with the task of reclaiming the vision of Jesus Christ and the New Testament models of inclusive congregations. The world has rightly judged the church a failure in addressing the

racial divide. Even so, we believe that multiracial congregations are God's plan for responding to racism
. . . we must quietly, intentionally, persistently, and
courageously begin to live our faith that God through
Jesus Christ can reconcile us across these entrenched
racial divides and that God has given each congregation, each individual, and each denomination the
ministry of reconciliation.[3]

Among Mennonites in particular, Racial/Ethnic members and
congregations bring the following qualities to the church:

1. A model of how to be "Anabaptist in the city"—something
   that few Mennonites in North America have experienced,
   even though the Anabaptist movement developed within
   urban contexts in Europe.
2. Youthfulness to an otherwise aging denomination that has
   fewer children than ever before.
3. An openness to charismatic expressions of the Holy Spirit
   that Mennonites have too often failed to nurture and have
   at times resisted.
4. A greater evangelical witness that is much needed in a
   denomination that has recognized its missional calling but
   whose members too often lack courage or passion to
   express in word and deed the good news of Jesus Christ.
5. The reality of poverty to remind more affluent Mennonites
   of injustices and inequities in the world and to challenge
   them to take more seriously the call of Jesus to abandon
   everything to follow him, including homeland security.
6. The three-fold combination of a charismatic spirituality, an
   active evangelical witness, and support for social justice
   that is nurtured in the daily challenges of urban violence,
   poverty, and injustice. Urban Mennonites, more so than
   others, hold together a deep commitment to the
   salvation of individuals as well as the transformation of
   society.

If the church is going to become truly multi-cultural, it will
mean sharing financial resources equitably, assigning Racial/Ethnic
members leadership roles across the church (including area conferences), connecting intentionally with geographic locations outside
the historic geographic enclaves of Mennonites and careful, patient
discernment of controversial theological and social issues. While

such efforts will take time, I believe the future of the denomination may rest—more than anything else—on the ability of the church to reconcile across racial and ethnic lines. For when the margins and middle of Mennonite Church USA disappear, shalom will come.

Other signs of the kingdom include:

- *Engaged members.* The high response rate of 76% among those who received a Mennonite Member Profile 2006 questionnaire suggests strong commitment by members to engage their church, even though they disagree on many issues.
- *Evangelism and peacemaking.* Mennonites believe that the church should be engaged in evangelism and peacemaking simultaneously. Despite assimilation, Mennonites value peacemaking as an ideal and want to see their church support such efforts alongside evangelistic outreach.
- *Stable marriages.* Mennonite marriages are more stable than those of other Americans, including conservative Protestants. In addition, Mennonite opposition to extramarital sex has increased. Models of stable marriages and families are much needed today, and Mennonites should take advantage of this strength in connecting with the broken marriages, families, and lives that affect so many of our neighbors, co-workers, and friends.
- *High rates of giving.* Mennonite rates of tithing and giving to the church and charitable organizations is much higher than among other Americans, including other Christians. While Mennonites have become more affluent, they also appear to be giving relatively freely.
- *Orthodox beliefs about Jesus.* Mennonites continue to hold orthodox teachings about Jesus—the virgin birth, the purpose of his death, and his physical resurrection. Beliefs about Jesus have changed little over thirty-five years.
- *Personal piety.* Mennonites have retained a kind of evangelical piety seen in the way that they talk about the closeness of their relationship with God, and with nearly all having received Jesus as Savior and Lord and most identifying themselves as "born again." If anything, this talk among Mennonites of a personal relationship with God has increased since 1972.
- *Women in ministry.* Mennonites have changed their views of gender roles, moving from a traditional view to one that is increasingly egalitarian. This has undoubtedly led to greater support for women in ministry.

The Church Itself as a Sign of God's Kingdom

Missional theologian Darrell Guder suggests that the church itself is a sign of God's kingdom. The church represents God's kingdom in three ways: (1) through loving and compassionate communities, (2) by serving the church and the world, and (3) by proclaiming the saving news of Jesus Christ.[4] Each is critical if local congregations are to recover an apostolic model of church that existed in the first century. These congregations, says Patrick Keifert, understood "themselves to be mission outposts with the mission of God; communities called, gathered, and sent in God's mission, the very movement of God toward the world."[5]

In the final question of the Mennonite Member Profile questionnaire, respondents were given an opportunity to share any final thoughts that they had about "Mennonite churches." Much of what they revealed in their open-ended comments reflected the realities of disruption and crisis addressed in this book. But many also shared moving testimonies of their experiences in local congregations—congregations that clearly reflect God's kingdom as loving, serving, and proclaiming communities. The responses of these members are evidence of "kingdom life" within Mennonite congregations, which, though struggling in the context of disruption and crisis, continue to reflect the reign of God in their journey together. While I separate the reflections of respondents below according to the three categories of loving, serving, and proclaiming communities, some of the comments can be applied to one or more of these categories.

Loving communities. As communities of faith, local congregations are characterized by their love for one another and for the world. Says Guder: "The church's love and unity holds ultimate significance for the world as the basis of the gospel's power and legitimacy."[6] Mennonite respondents said the following about their congregations:

- "I am glad there is a Mennonite church in my home city. The church is warm, giving, and provides me with the answers to my religious needs."

- "I'm glad there are churches in the Mennonite tradition where you can read authors the likes of Marcus Borg as well as Philip Yancey."
- "The Mennonite church I attend is a wonderful church. It has allowed me to have freedom to answer tough questions about God, the Bible, and religion in general. I truly appreciate this freedom which ultimately helps me better define my beliefs. I also compare this to my upbringing in another denomination where one was not necessarily challenged and given this 'space.'"
- "It is a wonderful place to find God and learn more about the Bible."
- "I appreciate the sense of community the Mennonite church offers."
- "Our congregation is a caring congregation with pastors that are very concerned about the members and also the community. They are delivering the word of God to BOTH."
- "We have a wonderful group of believers who support and pray for each other. We are flawed, fractured human beings held together by the love and sacrifice of Jesus Christ. That's it."
- "Mennonite churches have a family feeling—a place where one belongs and can grow. We need to learn how to better share this family with those outside our church walls."
- "I sincerely appreciate the opportunity to ask the hard questions of myself, my faith community and church, to reflect and discuss, without being summarily dismissed or condemned."
- "The best cooks in the world! Some of the nicest, kindest, sharing and caring people around."
- "Church has been good to us. When our child was dying, they were there with food, baby-sitting, companionship, financial support."
- "I get a warm, fuzzy feeling in my church. I can feel love all around me."
- "I feel my church meets my needs. They supported me during my cancer and pray for my unsaved husband. The church family seems to be the Mennonite motto."
- "The Mennonite church has been a place to learn about Jesus and his love to me and the world. Its people have modeled eternal values for me. I have been challenged in many areas of life to pray and serve the God of the universe who created

man to glorify him! It has also given us a challenge to help lost souls find a safe haven in the blood of Jesus shed for our salvation. Jesus is coming again!"

- I'm so thankful that my parents sent us to a Mennonite church when we were growing up. I am who I am because of the teachings, caring people, the seeds that those committed saints sowed into my life. They introduced me and my family to Jesus and taught us godly principles. Praise God for them!"

- "My local church has grown into receiving members from other denominational backgrounds, affirming gifts, offering opportunities for significant involvement at all levels of church life. I have felt very welcomed."

- "I attend a home-based Mennonite fellowship (shared leadership, meet in homes) with about twenty to thirty members. It is a concept I would like to catch on in the wider Mennonite church."

- "I love the congregation. I have been with the church since 1988 and faithful each week with God's help. I first came in 1960 but became ill and left, but I'm back to stay. Thank God."

- "The spirit of humility, community and cooperation in the Mennonite church is rare among evangelical churches today."

- "So far I have been very pleased and pleasantly surprised with how wonderful our new (relatively new) church is. I have only been going there for over a year. My wife and two sons (out of seven children) joined. I like it and may join officially in the future."

- "I love our church—the values, the fact that it is biblical, the community and relationships are important."

- "I'm grateful to be a part of a church that has supported, nurtured, and guided me through my seventy-five years!"

Serving communities. As communities of faith, local congregations are also servants whose impulse is to "respond to the whole range of need in humanity and in creation." This impulse is patterned after Jesus himself who "was predisposed to be interrupted, even from his focal point of preaching, whenever hunger, sickness, demonic oppression, the grip of sin, social ostracism, or death crossed his path."[7] Again, the responses of members to their congregations and their experiences in the broader church reflect such service:

- "Having been in other denominations (Methodist, Presbyterian, Charismatic) being in the Mennonite church feels most like home because of the stance it takes on pro-life issues in more than just the abortion debate; its stand on nonviolence, peace and justice issues, simple living, ministering to the poor, high view of scripture, the ministry of ALL believers—not just pastors."
- "I am very grateful to have discovered the Mennonite church and rediscovered the Gospels and Sermon on the Mount. Real Christians need to live it out and follow Jesus as example."
- "Living in an urban setting has made me realize the radical declaration peace and nonviolence are in an age of violence and destruction. The Mennonite church has a challenge to maintain this message of the gospel."
- "I think one of the greatest messages the Mennonite church has to offer the wider ecumenical church (and the world) is Christ's teaching about peace."
- "Mennonite churches do a good job of serving others at home and away from home."
- "I wouldn't choose to go to any other church. I appreciate all the volunteering and service efforts that the churches are doing."
- "I am grateful for the Mennonite/Anabaptist expression in the broader Christian church and in service to our world."
- "We have a lot going for us—the churches I've been a part of over the past twenty-five years have been respected for our stand on service, peace, and justice. The community was grateful for the witness presented by Mennos!"
- "Not growing up in the Mennonite faith, what drew me to my current congregation was the people, all the compassion they had for their community, for the unsaved, and for devastation in the world. Then, as I became more familiar with the Mennonite confession of faith, it began to challenge me and began to understand the positions that make the Mennonite faith different."
- "The church has been a strong beacon of light in a rather dim world."
- "I am pleased and feel blessed to be a part of our church,

which is active around the world helping people who suffer and have real needs."

Proclaiming communities. Finally, local congregations that discover their missional calling will proclaim the good news of Jesus Christ: "The church's being and doing are irretrievably tied to its proclaiming. . . . The declaration of the message entrusted to the church gives substantial content and definition to what its being and doing signify. . . . to refrain from proclamation leaves all else anonymous, ambiguous, and subject to misreading the situation. . . . Proclamation is inevitable if our being and doing signify anything at all about the presence of God's reign."[8] Mennonite members both applauded their church for its efforts to proclaim the gospel and challenged the church to do more such proclamation:

- "Mennonite churches [consist of] missionary people. We all like to go out in the world and be servants to all in need. . . . You preach the good word, and most of all you live the word. . . . I know all this because it took two people who came knocking on my door asking if we would like to send our children to summer Bible school. We did, and here I am forty years later. I am so thankful and grateful for teaching the Word to my children and me and my husband. I've been a widow for thirty years. Our church family has been good."
- "I thank God for the Mennonite church for bringing the gospel of Jesus Christ to the country of Belize and other countries."
- "I am thankful the Mennonite church has become more diverse of race/culture and affirming church planting ministries."
- "I like the diversity that is taking place at home and around the world and the missional emphasis in the denomination."
- "They are reaching out to the community to draw more people to the Lord."
- "I appreciate the involvement of the church in outreach to the community."
- "Most generally we're 'right on' (in line with Jesus' teachings). We need to make sure we don't become complacent/content and quit serving and discerning God's will for us.

We need to take time to share the good news of peace with others."

- "Move to the city—God loves the city—early Christianity was born in the city. By 2007, half of the world's population will live in the city."
- "I think Mennonite churches need to be more relevant to the communities they are in. It doesn't make sense to have people dying and suffering in your own neighborhood and not doing anything about it."
- "In my view we do a pretty good job helping each other within our own churches but could improve our outreach to our nearby communities."
- "Church planting—larger churches need to give all types of support to the new church planting."
- "I have a strong opinion that when we leave our home church on Sunday, we enter into the mission field. I would like to see more mission workers sent into the inner cities to work with and role model to these neighborhoods."
- "We need to be able to reach out to the unchurched even if it means starting a soup kitchen, for example. There is an awful lot of need out there! We are too happy to just be the same from year to year. However, if we don't find a way to grow (as a church) we will surely die out."
- "I choose to continue to worship at a Mennonite church as the peace issue is still promoted. Also souls are still being saved."
- "I love the Mennonite church. We have so much to offer our communities—salvation, stability (good foundation), serving, love, caring, peace, etc. May we continue to work on evangelism to the unsaved."
- "This church has shown me more acceptance, love, kindness, caring than any other church. . . . I felt comfortable and accepted enough to know it was okay to invite a ragged, poor Apache Indian man and his wife to church with me this week. They were both blown away by the loving kindness shown to them by our church. They did not feel judged and said they did not feel any hypocrisy in our church. I think it was probably the first time he has ever heard the gospel."
- "I feel Mennonite churches are doing a better job of reaching others for Christ than they did twenty-five to fifty years

ago. Our leaders have helped us in this vision. Praise the Lord for Christian leaders who empower their congregations to serve the Lord!!"

Conclusion

In Jeremiah chapter thirty-two and in advance of the destruction of Jerusalem, God commanded Jeremiah to buy a field and to put the copy of the deed in a clay jar, as a sign from God that "houses, fields, and vineyards will again be bought in this land." Despite the judgment that God would bring on Judah by Babylon, God still promised:

> "As I have brought great calamity on this people, so I will give them all the prosperity I have promised them. Once more fields will be bought in this land of which you say, 'It is a desolate waste, without men or animals, for it has been handed over to the Babylonians.' Fields will be bought for silver, and deeds will be signed, sealed and witnessed in the territory of Benjamin, in the villages around Jerusalem . . . because I will restore their fortunes," declares the LORD. (Jeremiah 32:42-44)

The apostle Paul, when referring to God's people in 2 Corinthians 4, whether intentionally or not, picks up on God's promise to Jeremiah when he compares our current predicament as God's people with clay jars:

> But we have this treasure in jars of clay to show that this all-surpassing power is from God and not from us. We are hard pressed on every side, but not crushed; perplexed, but not in despair; persecuted, but not abandoned; struck down, but not destroyed. We always carry around in our body the death of Jesus, so that the life of Jesus may also be revealed in our body. . . . So then, death is at work in us, but life is at work in you. (vv. 7-11, 12)

As Mennonites journeying toward God's reign, we must have faith to affirm that God has deposited within us—individuals, families, local congregations, area conferences, and denomination—all of the treasure needed to accomplish God's missional purposes. Though we are hard pressed and perplexed, though we are in the midst of crisis and disruption, though there seems to be more change than stability—yet, we are not crushed, we are not in despair, we are not abandoned, and we are not destroyed. For the life of Jesus Christ has been deposited within us and will yet be revealed in ways that most of us have not even begun to imagine.

It is likely that Mennonite Church USA will look substantially different by the time of the next member profile. On the one hand, if local congregations increasingly reflect God's reign, such changes will bring new members who will have more questions rather than fewer about what it means to be Anabaptist, and they will show less loyalty rather than more to any one denomination. On the other hand, if congregations fail to be loving, serving, and proclaiming communities, the disruption seen in the data of Mennonite Member Profile 2006 will continue with a decline in members, further erosion of spiritual vitality, and the loss of any effective witness to the world. If this occurs the denomination itself will eventually disappear.

Either outcome should cause followers of Jesus Christ to recognize that the church as a sign of God's kingdom extends beyond denominational boundaries to include all persons—regardless of race, ethnicity, age, gender, social status, or denomination—who desire to belong to communities that love one another, are committed to serving the world, and are renewed in their proclamation of Jesus Christ as the best news that history has ever heard.

The journey toward God's reign is unpredictable, and the question of how long any particular denomination survives is probably less important than whether you and I are part of Christian communities that signal God's reign. The uncertainty of our predicament is not cause for despair but rather for celebration. If the chaos of the fifteenth and sixteenth centuries could birth the Anabaptist movement from a rag-tag band of Roman Catholic and Reformed believers, God can surely renew their descendants (genealogical and spiritual) in a way that blesses not only one denomination in North America in the twenty-first century but the whole world throughout all time and eternity.

Faithful journeying toward the reign of God means addressing the disruption that we feel and the chaos we fear, and it means over-coming our tendencies to "default" to our previous understandings of the church under Christendom. It will also mean opening our-selves to the movement of God's Spirit in anxiety-producing ways. But our faithfulness in doing so will inevitably lead us all to one place—to the throne of the Lion and of the Lamb, singing in uni-son (or even four-part harmony) as we arrive:

> You are worthy to take the scroll and to open its seals, for you were slaughtered and by your blood you ransomed for God saints from every tribe and language and people and nation; you have made them to be a kingdom and priests serving our God, and they will reign on earth. . . . To the one seated on the throne and to the Lamb be blessing and honor and glory and might forever and forever! . . . Amen. (Revelation 5:9-10, 13-14 NRSV)

Come, Lord Jesus!

Notes

1: Road Signs and Guideposts

1. All of these congregations belong to area conferences that are part of Mennonite Church USA.

2. Church Member Profile I was conducted in 1972 by J. Howard Kauffman and Leland Harder. Church Member Profile II in 1989 was led by J. Howard Kauffman, Leland Harder, and Leo Driedger. The results of these two projects are reported in *Anabaptists: Four Centuries Later* (1975) by J. Howard Kauffman and Leland Harder, *The Mennonite Mosaic: Identity and Modernization* (1991) by J. Howard Kauffman and Leo Driedger (1991), and *Doors to Open, Doors to Close* by Leland Harder and J. Howard Kauffman (1993).

3. Fewer members and congregations are part of Mennonite Church USA in 2007 than when Mennonite Member Profile 2006 was initiated in 2005. In addition, a realignment of area conferences resulted in the dissolution of Rocky Mountain area conference and the creation of Mountain States area conference. Unless otherwise noted, our discussion of the denomination's area conferences, congregations, and members is based upon the databases that we received when we began the study.

4. Pastors received a letter inviting their congregation to participate in the study. Nearly 85% agreed to do so. Those congregations who declined or failed to respond were replaced, resulting in a final sample of 120 congregations.

5. The two earlier member profiles (Church Member Profile I and Church Member Profile II) included five Anabaptist denominations in Canada and the United States: the Mennonite Brethren, the Brethren in Christ, the General Conference Mennonite Church, the (Old) Mennonite Church, and the Evangelical Mennonite Church. They also included congregational members thirteen years of age and older. In this book, data from the earlier member profiles will include only members eighteen years of age and older from the former General Conference Mennonite Church and the (Old) Mennonite Church in the United States. The sample size for the 1972 profile is 1,382 members and for the 1989 profile is 1,110 members. Due to the complexity of analysis with five different samples (1972, 1989, 2006, Racial/Ethnic, and Pastor) throughout this book, I do not provide confidence intervals when comparing differences across

them. In many cases, differences are sizeable. Where they are not, I attempt to use language that suggests caution in drawing conclusions about their differences.

6. This is an adjusted rate that does not include members of the sample who were deceased or who could not be contacted. For analysis of the member data (not including the urban Racial/Ethnic or pastor samples), two weights were created for gender and congregation. These weights compensate for disproportionate congregation and gender response rates with respect to the population of all members of Mennonite Church USA. The weights make the sample similar to the larger population in terms of congregation and gender non-response in order to allow for representative statistical analysis.

7. The number of Racial/Ethnic congregations and members is actually higher, since the denominational database of these congregations provided by Mennonite Church USA in 2005 included a number of omissions—congregations apparently not reported as Racial/Ethnic by their own congregations or area conferences. Combining the number of Racial/Ethnic members in Racial/Ethnic congregations with those in predominantly white congregations, I estimate that the membership of Mennonite Church USA is nearly 15% Racial/Ethnic. The largest proportion of Racial/Ethnic congregations are Latino/Hispanic (46%), followed by African-American (35%), Asian (11%), and Native American (8%). African-Americans, however, have the largest membership, representing 52% of Racial/Ethnic members in the denomination (one-third of these attend a single congregation—Calvary Community Church in Hampton, Virginia), followed by Latino/Hispanic members (35%), Asian members (9%), and Native American members (4%).

8. In each urban area, project partners distributed and collected the surveys—Yvonne Platts and Freeman Miller, representing the Philadelphia Urban Ministries Partnership (PUMP) in Philadelphia, Rodolfo Jimenez, who serves with Mennonite Central Committee in Chicago, and Valentina Satvedi representing the Center for Anabaptist Leadership in Los Angeles. The effective work of these partners was critical to the overall response of congregations in these urban areas. Based on consultations with project partners, the urban Racial/Ethnic questionnaire was redesigned and shortened from the full-length member profile used in the representative sample. In addition, the questionnaire for each urban area included specific questions suggested by the project partner for that area, resulting in three slightly different (though sharing a common core of questions) surveys, each translated into Spanish. Twenty-one Racial/Ethnic congregations participated, including multi-Racial/Ethnic, African-American, Latino/Hispanic, Vietnamese, Chinese, African immigrant, and Indonesian. Combining the Racial/Ethnic members in the urban sample (300) with Racial/Ethnic members who were part of the representative member profile (175) yielded a total of 475 Racial/Ethnic members in Mennonite Member Profile 2006. The Racial/Ethnic distribution of these combined samples was 26% African-American, 25% Latino/Hispanic, 25% Asian, 4% Native American, 6% African, 9% mixed, and

7% other. While the findings from this sample do not necessarily represent all Racial/Ethnic members in Mennonite Church USA, this data is the best quantitative information ever about Racial/Ethnic Mennonites in the United States.

9. References to "member" findings in this book are based on the representative sample of members in Mennonite Member Profile 2006 (2,216 respondents) and references to "Racial/Ethnic members" will typically include the 175 Racial/Ethnic members from the representative member sample as well as the 300 members in the special urban Racial/Ethnic sample (except for a number questions that were not asked in the urban survey).

10. Walter Brueggemann, 2006.

11. Brueggemann, 1986:7.

12. Darrell L. Guder, 1998:2.

13. Sociologists tend to define evangelical Protestants as those who ascribe to a literal interpretation of Scripture, identify Jesus Christ as their personal Lord and Savior, and emphasize evangelism to the unsaved. Examples of evangelicals include various Baptist groups, the Christian and Missionary Alliance, the Assemblies of God, as well as independent, nondenominational churches. The mainline Protestant denominations (sometimes also called the "Oldline" by sociologists) include Presbyterian, Lutheran, Methodist, Episcopalian, and United Church of Christ denominations, among others.

14. For a discussion of the Mennonite "third way" see Paul M. Lederach, *A Third Way*.

15. John Roth, C. Henry Smith Lecture, April 5, 2005:7.

16. Brueggemann, 2006:189-98.

17. Lesslie Newbigin, 1987.

18. My own understanding of missional church reflected throughout this book has been shaped substantially through the teaching and writing of Patrick Keifert (2006) and Alan Roxburgh (2005, 2006), particularly through the Partnership for Missional Church. Partnership for Missional Church of Church Innovations, Inc. is a journey of spiritual discernment for congregations interested in pursuing their missional vocation. Others who have engaged the missional conversation that began with Lesslie Newbigin include Lois Barrett (2004), David Bosch, (1991), Darrell Guder (1998), George R. Hunsberger and Craig Van Gelder (1996).

2: God's People Then

1. Frederick Buechner, 2006:37-39.

2. Brueggemann, 1986:ix.

3. By biblical narrative I am referring to an understanding of the Bible that acknowledges a cultural, social, and historical context for the text as well as an appreciation for the individuality of the one writing the text. In this way, the Bible has a greater chance of becoming a living story into which all of us can insert our own contexts and persons, and out of which we can still hear God speak.

4. Brueggemann, 1986:ix.

5. Brueggemann, 1998:xiii.

6. Elmer Martens, 1986:17; chronology of Jeremiah's life also adapted from Martens.

7. Brueggemann, 1998:xi-xii.

8. Martens, 1986.

9. Brueggemann, 1986.

10. Martens, 1986:25.

11. Abraham Heschel in Martens, 1986:26-27.

12. Martens, 1986:26.

13. Brueggemann, 1998:x.

14. Brueggemann, 2006:194.

15. Brueggemann, 1986:195.

16. Martens, 1986:26.

3: God's People Now

1. *Mennonite Yearbook & Directory* (various dates). Scottdale, Pa.: Mennonite Publishing House, 1971 and 1990-1991.

2. The number of members in Mennonite Church USA has declined since the beginning of Mennonite Member Profile 2006 by nearly more than two thousand—from 111,507 to 109,000. Recent congregational and membership data reported in this book are based on Mennonite Church USA data provided to Mennonite Member Profile 2006 and Mennonite Church USA 2005 and 2007 directories.

3. Diether G. Lichdi and Loretta Kreider, editors, 1990; Mennonite World Conference news release, November 22, 2006.

4. Mark Chaves, 2004.

5. Regions were created according to the U.S. Census designation as follows: East=Connecticut, Maine, Massachusetts, New Hampshire, New Jersey, New York, Pennsylvania, Rhode Island, Vermont; Midwest=Illinois, Indiana, Iowa, Kansas, Michigan, Minnesota, Ohio, Wisconsin, North Dakota, Nebraska, South Dakota; West=Arizona, California, Colorado, Idaho, Montana, Nevada, New Mexico, Oregon, Utah, Washington, Wyoming; South=Alabama, Arkansas, Delaware, Florida, Georgia, Kentucky, Louisiana, Maryland, Mississippi, North Carolina, South Carolina, Tennessee, Texas, Virginia, West Virginia, Oklahoma.

6. *Mennonite Yearbook & Directory*. Scottdale, Pa.: Mennonite Publishing House, 1992. No equivalent Racial/Ethnic data is available for the General Conference Mennonite Church.

7. Baylor University, 2005. The Baylor Religion Survey, Waco, TX: Baylor Institute for Studies of Religion.

8. The median age in 2006 was also fifty-four years.

9. Andrew Greeley and Michael Hout, 2006:110.

10. Based on data from the 2000 U.S. Census (www.censusscope.org /us/chart_age.html)

11. Jackson Dykman, 2006.
12. Kauffman and Driedger, 1991.
13. Dykman, 2006.
14. Greeley and Hout, 2006.
15. Based on data from the 2000 U.S. Census
(www.censusscope.org/us/chart_income.html.

4: The Call

1. Brueggemann, 2003.
2. Martens, 1986:18-19.
3. Greeley and Hout, 2006.
4. Chester Wenger, 1964:73.

5: God's Words—Then and Now

1. Brueggemann, 1997.
2. Brueggemann, 2000:1-2.
3. Patrick Keifert, 2006.
4. Alan Roxburgh and Fred Romanuk, 2006:34.
5. Brueggemann, 2000:8.
6. Brueggemann, 2000:9.
7. The term "global south" generally refers to developing and under-developed countries of Asia, Latin America, and Africa.
8. Greeley and Hout, 2006.
9. Ibid.
10. Ibid.
11. Ibid.
12. Ibid.
13. Peter Berger, 1967.
14. Ronald J. Sider, 2005.

6: Homeland Security

1. John L. Ruth, 2003.
2. Sider, 2005.
3. Sider, 2005:21-22.
4. *Wikipedia.* en.wikipedi.org/wiki/Homeownship_in_the_United_States
5. Greeley and Hout, 2006.
6. Sider, 2005:51-52.
7. Curtiss Paul DeYoung et. al, 2003:182.
8. Greeley and Hout, 2006
9. Greeley and Hout, 2006:72.
10. Greeley and Hout, 2006:73.
11. Roth, April 5, 2005:7.
12. Greeley and Hout, 2006:83-84.
13. Greeley and Hout, 2006:23.

7: 587 BC—The Fall

1. Earl Creps, 2006:17-18.
2. Samuel Moore Shoemaker, 1967.
3. Alan J. Roxburgh, 2006:74.
4. Ibid.
5. Among other writings by Lesslie Newbigin see "The Cultural Captivity of Western Christianity as a Challenge to a Missionary Church," 1994:66-79.
6. For a more extensive discussion of the fall of Christendom see Patrick Keifert, 2006.
7. Sider, 2005:86.
8. Greeley and Hout, 2006:110.
9. Robert N. Bellah et. al., 1985.
10. Greeley and Hout, 2006.
11. Brueggemann, 1986:4.

8: Exiled in Babylon

1. Roxburgh, 2006:74.
2. Sider, 2005:12-13, 57, 85.
3. Ibid., 104.
4. Helmut Harder, 1997:140.
5. John D. Roth, 2005:126.
6. Ibid., 140.
7. Harder, 1997:138.
8. Roth, 2005:104-5.
9. Greeley and Hout, 2006.
10. Ibid.
11. Ibid.
12. Sider, 2005
13. Ibid., 130-31.

9: The Journey Home

1. Donald B. Kraybill, 2003.
2. Roth, 2005:90-91.
3. DeYoung et. al, 2003:183-84.
4. Guder, 1998.
5. Keifert, 2006:5.
6. Guder, 1998:104.
7. Ibid., 105.
8. Ibid., 107.

Bibliography

Barrett, Lois, 2004. *Treasure in Clay Jars: Patterns in Missional Faithfulness*. The Gospel and Our Culture Series. Grand Rapids, Mich.: Wm. B. Eerdmans.

Bellah, Robert N., Richard Madsen, William M. Sullivan, and Ann Swidler. 1985. *Habits of the Heart: Individualism and Commitment in American Life*. Los Angeles: University of California Press.

Berger, Peter. 1967. *The Sacred Canopy*. New York: Anchor Books.

Bosch, David J. 1991. *Transforming Mission: Paradigm Shifts in Theology of Mission*. American Society of Missiology Series, no. 16. Maryknoll, N.Y.: Orbis Books.

Brueggemann, Walter. 2006. *Like Fire in the Bones: Listening for the Prophetic Word in Jeremiah*. Minneapolis: Fortress Press.

———. 2003. *An Introduction to the Old Testament: The Canon and Christian Imagination*. Louisville, Ky.: Westminster John Knox Press.

———. 2000. *Texts that Linger Words that Explode: Listening to Prophetic Voices*. Minneapolis: Fortress Press.

———. 1998. *A Commentary on Jeremiah: Exile and Homecoming*. Grand Rapids, Mich.: Wm. B. Eerdmans.

———. 1997. *Cadences of Home: Preaching Among Exiles*. Louisville, Ky.: Westminster John Knox Press.

———. 1986. *Hopeful Imagination: Prophetic Voices in Exile*. Philadelphia: Fortress Press.

Buechner, Frederick. 2006. *Secrets in the Dark: A Life in Sermons*. San Francisco: HarperSanFrancisco.

Chaves, Mark. 2004. *Congregations in America*. Cambridge, Mass.: Harvard University Press.

Creps, Earl. 2006. *Off-Road Disciplines: Spiritual Adventures of Missional Leaders*. San Francisco: Jossey-Bass.

DeYoung, Curtiss Paul, et al. 2003. *United By Faith: The Multiracial Congregation as an Answer to the Problem of Race*. New York: Oxford University Press.

Dykman, Jackson. 2006. "America by the Numbers." *Time*. October 30, 2006:41-54.

Greeley, Andrew, and Michael Hout. 2006. *The Truth About Conservative Christians: What They Think and What They Believe*. Chicago: University of Chicago Press.

Guder, Darrell L., editor. 1998. *Missional Church: A Vision for the Sending of the Church in North America*. The Gospel and Our Culture Series. Grand Rapids, Mich.: Wm. B. Eerdmans.

Harder, Helmut. 1997. *Understanding the Faith from a Mennonite Perspective: A Study Guide*. Newton, Kansas: Faith &Life Press.

Harder, Leland, and J. Howard Kauffman. 1993. *Doors to Open, Doors to Close: The Discerning People of God*. Scottdale, Pa.: Herald Press.

Heschel, Abraham. 1962. *The Prophets*. New York: Harper & Row.

Jackson, E., editor. 1994. *A Word in Season: Perspectives on Christian World Missions*. Grand Rapids, Mich./Edinburgh: Eerdmans/Saint Andrews Press.

Jenkins, Philip. 2006. *The New Faces of Christianity: Believing the Bible in the Global South*. New York: Oxford University Press.

Kauffman, J. Howard, and Leland Harder. 1975. *Anabaptists: Four Centuries Later*. Scottdale, Pa.: Herald Press.

Kauffman, J. Howard, and Leo Driedger. 1991. *The Mennonite Mosaic: Identity and Modernization*. Scottdale, Pa.: Herald Press.

Keifert, Patrick. 1992. *Welcoming the Stranger: A Public Theology of Worship and Evangelism*. Minneapolis, Minn.: Fortress Press.

———. 2006. *We Are Here Now: A New Missional Era*. Eagle, Idaho: Allelon Publishing.

Kraybill, Donald B. 2003. *The Upside-Down Kingdom*. 3rd ed. Scottdale, Pa.: Herald Press.

Lederach, Paul. M. 1980. *A Third Way*. Scottdale, Pa.: Herald Press.

Lichdi, Diether G., and Loretta Kreider, editors. 1990. *Mennonite World Handbook: Mennonites in Global Witness*, Carol Stream, Ill.: Mennonite World Conference.

Newbigin, Lesslie. 1987. "Can the West be Converted?" *Evangelical Review of Theology*, 11:355-68.

———. 1994. "The Cultural Captivity of Western Christianity as a Challenge to a Missionary Church," in *A Word in Season: Perspectives on Christian World Missions*. Grand Rapids, Mich./Edinburgh: Eerdmans/Saint Andrews Press, 66-79.

Martens, Elmer A. 1986. *Jeremiah*. Believers Church Bible Commentary Series. Scottdale, Pa: Herald Press.

Roxburgh, Alan J. 2006. *The Sky is Falling: Leaders Lost in Transition*. Eagle, Idaho: Allelon.

———. 2006. "What is Missional Church?" Summer Institute Workbook. Eagle, Idaho: Allelon Publishing.

Roxburgh, Alan J., and Fred Romanuk. 2006. *The Missional Leader: Equipping Your Church to Reach a Changing World*. San Francisco: Jossey-Bass.

Roth, John D. 2005. *Beliefs: Mennonite Faith and Practice*. Scottdale, Pa.: Herald Press.

———. 2005. "Called to One Peace: Christian Faith and Political Witness in a Divided Culture." C. Henry Smith Lecture at Goshen College, April 5, 2005. Available on the Internet at www.goshen.edu/news/pressarchive/o4-11-05-smith-folo.html

Ruth, John L. 2003. *The Earth Is the Lord's: A Narrative History of the Lancaster Mennonite Conference*. Scottdale, Pa.: Herald Press.

Shoemaker, Samuel Moore. 1967. "I Stand by the Door" in *I Stand by the Door: The Life of Samuel Shoemaker*, by Helen Smith Shoemaker. Waco, Tex.: Word Books.

Sider, Ronald J. 2005. *The Scandal of the Evangelical Conscience*. Grand Rapids, Mich.: Baker Books.

Wenger, Chester. 1964. "The Church's Task" in *Called to Be Sent: Fifty Years in Mission,* edited by Paul N. Kraybill. Scottdale, Pa.: Herald Press, pp. 66-73.

Weston, Paul, ed. 2006 *Lesslie Newbigin: Missionary Theologian*. Grand Rapids, Mich.: Wm. B. Eerdmans.

The Author

Conrad L. Kanagy is associate professor of sociology at Elizabethtown (Pennsylvania) College. He is a consultant to congregations and served as pastor at Elizabethtown Mennonite Church from 2000 to 2005. He holds graduate degrees in rural sociology from Penn State University. He is the co-author, with Donald B. Kraybill, of *Riddles of Human Society* (1990). Kanagy was born in Covington, Kentucky, and grew up in Belleville, Pennsylvania. He and his wife and son live in Elizabethtown.

"The immense value of being sensitive to what 'the Spirit says to the churches' was and is of vital importance. It is in this understanding that Conrad Kanagy provides both biblical and analytical insights on where Mennonites have been, where we are currently as a denomination, and where we are moving to as a people belonging to God. As in the past, we can simply reject the prophetic utterances offered in this book as foolishness and ignore the seasonal changes already impacting us. Or perhaps we can seriously discern the seasonal changes upon us and all the challenges and opportunities they present. *Road Signs for the Journey* offers a guide that prayerfully positions us, both individually and congregationally, for the harvest that our Lord and Savior Jesus Christ promises!"

—Leonard Dow, pastor of Oxford Circle Mennonite Church, Philadelphia

"Conrad Kanagy shows how sociology can work together with theology. This book takes stock of where we are as a Mennonite people and looks at what this means for our identity and the missional character of the church. Can we take the information gained from a questionnaire and use it as a basis for listening more carefully to God's call and acting on it? The book is a good antidote to the notion that one has to choose between evangelism and peacemaking, or between identity and mission. We CAN be different from the surrounding cultures and yet engage those cultures with the gospel."

—Lois Barrett, Associated Mennonite Biblical Seminary

"Conrad Kanagy is not only a good sociologist able to read the signs of the times, he is also a deeply caring and wise pastoral leader. The research and findings of this book should be read by all those in Mennonite Church USA who are about what God may be about in this movement at this moment in time. Indeed, the times are a-changin' and Kanagy's work provides a well-documented mapping of these changes, as well as ways to engage the challenges that now lie on the road ahead."

—Alan J. Roxburgh, author of *The Sky is Falling!?! Leaders Lost in Transition*

"Rarely does a social scientist dare enter the theological and cultural world of the church as Conrad Kanagy has so helpfully done. Weaving together strands of compiled data, biblical prophecy, and contextual insights, Kanagy reveals the fabric of Mennonite Church USA today. Her strength and resilience, her delicate precariousness, and her purpose in the world all come into focus as we are challenged with the church's task for the future. This book is a gift—and a wake-up call—for the church today."

>   —Janet Plenert, Executive Secretary of
>   Mennonite Church Canada Witness

"Conrad Kanagy as a scholar shows us the sociological road signs of who we are as a denomination. But in this book he is also a pastor, and like the prophet Jeremiah points to the road signs of who we want to be as God's people. I highly recommend this book to Mennonite Church USA congregations for study."

>   —Roy W. Williams, Moderator, Mennonite Church USA

Also available DVD and CD of printable materials

Resources
for the **Journey**
A Profile of Mennonite Church USA

This DVD and CD resource package can help congregations discern God's plans and purposes for God's people.

The materials are based on *Road Signs for the Journey: A Profile of Mennonite Church USA*, by Conrad L. Kanagy. The DVD features seven video modules that can be used in worship, small groups, or Sunday School classes. The modules can be used individually or together over a seven-week period.

The CD contains printable resources including:
- Daily devotional suggestions
- Worship resources, including scripture and song suggestions, and sermon outlines
- Small group and Sunday school curriculum, including leader's guides, survey questions from the 2006 Mennonite Member Profile, and reflection questions

Produced by David Sollenberger
Written by Conrad L. Kanagy
Executive producers: Donald B. Kraybill and Conrad L. Kanagy

To order or request information, please call Herald Press,
Scottdale, Pennsylvania 1-800-245-7894, and
Waterloo, Ontario 1-800-631-6535
or visit www.heraldpress.com.

ISBN: 978-0-8361-9376-3